PENGUIN HANDBOOK PH 125

The Penguin Dictionary of Cookery

Rosemary Hume and Muriel Downes both had a sound practical training in cookery before the war, and went on to gain wide experience of writing, demonstrating, and teaching. They have been concerned for some fourteen years with the running and development of the Cordon Bleu School of Cookery, of which they are directors and co-principals. Together they are the authors of *Penguin Cordon Bleu Cookery*.

The Penguin Dictionary of

COOKERY

Rosemary Hume and Muriel Downes

Penguin Books

Penguin Books Ltd, Harmondsworth, Middlesex, England
Penguin Books Inc., 7110 Ambassador Road, Baltimore, Maryland 21207, U.S.A.
Penguin Books Australia Ltd, Ringwood, Victoria, Australia

—

First published 1966
Reprinted 1968

—

—

Made and printed in Great Britain
by Cox & Wyman Ltd, London, Fakenham and Reading
Set in Monotype Times

Agar-Agar. Made from seaweed and used to set jellies, cold soufflés, etc., where an animal extract such as gelatine is forbidden. Also used in medicine.

Aigrette. A batter savoury. The most usual are cheese aigrettes and anchovy aigrettes. The former are small quantities of cheese chou pastry, fried in deep fat until well puffed and golden-brown; the latter, fillets of anchovy dipped in fritter batter and fried also in deep fat.

Aioli. A garlic MAYONNAISE from Provence served with boiled fish, shellfish, boiled vegetables, and cold meats. Three or four cloves of garlic are crushed and blended with the egg-yolks before the olive oil is worked in. The mayonnaise is sharpened with lemon juice or vinegar in the usual way.

Allspice or Jamaican Pepper (*Pimenta officinalis*). It is called 'allspice' as the flavour is that of several spices, cinnamon, cloves, and nutmeg. Allspice resembles a large brown peppercorn and may, like peppercorns, be ground in a mill. It is useful for flavouring grills and other meat dishes. Not to be confused with mixed spice.

Allumettes. Match-shaped pieces; e.g. fried potatoes, *pommes allumettes*, or a *pâtisserie* consisting of slices of puff pastry spread with royal icing and baked.

Almond. There are two distinct varieties of almond, sweet and bitter, the former being more frequently used. One bitter almond among fifty or more sweet is considered adequate as a flavouring. A larger proportion than this, as well as being unpleasant, is poisonous. Of the sweet almonds there are two varieties, Jordan and Valencia. Jordan almonds (from Malaga) are the most expensive and are considered the finest. Long in shape, they are used mostly for dessert. Valencias are flat, and broad in comparison. They are used for cakes, pastries, and marzipan.

Aluminium Foil. A valuable asset in the modern kitchen, foil can be used when any food for refrigeration or for cooking is to be kept sealed from the air or from direct heat. Foil is best for covering food for steaming or to conserve moisture, rather than for use in roasting where direct heat and constant basting are necessary.

Amyli. See TAMARIND.

Anchovy. Small silvery fish imported chiefly from the Mediterranean and preserved in brine or oil. Fillets of anchovy in small tins are the best buy for the average household and are used mostly for savouries and salads. The whole fish or fillets may be soaked in milk to remove excess salt. Anchovy essence is useful as a flavouring for sauces, devils, and savoury butters.

Angel Cake. A cake, American in origin, made with egg-whites, sugar, and flour. Angel cake is white in colour and is baked in a special tin or MOULD.

Angelica (*Archangelica officinalis*). A handsome plant classified as a herb, the stalks of which are candied and used as a decoration for sweets and iced cakes. It has a pleasant flavour, and a little chopped angelica mixes well with the fruit in a plum cake.

Angels on Horseback. One of the better-known savouries, these are oysters wrapped in thin rashers of bacon and baked or grilled until crisp. Served on hot buttered toast.

Angler Fish. Little known in England, but caught off the French coasts. It is used mainly as an ingredient of BOUILLABAISSE.

Aniseed. The oil from the herb anise (*Pimpinella anisum*). Very pungent and used for flavouring sweets, e.g. aniseed balls, and apéritifs, e.g. anisette.

Apple. Apples are divided into two main groups, eating or dessert apples and cooking apples. They are essentially an English fruit, and many varieties are grown in England, maturing from August to late March. Cooking apples are sharply acid, and it is this quality that makes the flesh soft and pulpy when cooked. Some eating apples cook well, especially the pippins as they are mildly acid in flavour; when cooked these give a rich buttery pulp suitable for a flan or cake filling. They are also ideal for compotes or for poaching whole, as in syrup they go soft and semi-transparent and yet retain their shape. A sweet apple, e.g. Worcester Pearmain, will be tough and leathery if cooked. Among the varieties grown commercially are:

DESSERT OR EATING APPLES

Beauty of Bath. Season August. A small, attractive apple, heavily streaked with red on a yellow skin. The shape is round, slightly flat; and the flesh white, tinged with pink. It does not keep well.

Worcester Pearmain. Season September and October. A conical apple with a deep eye. Bright crimson on one side and greenish-yellow on the other. Crisp white flesh.

Cox's Orange Pippin. Season November to late January. The best-known and perhaps the best of the eating apples. Medium to small in size, greenish-yellow on one side, and with a pretty red flush on the other. The flesh is creamy yellow and crisp, and has a rich aromatic flavour. A test of perfect ripeness is that the pips rattle when the apple is shaken.

Laxton's Epicure and Laxton's Superb. Season September to November. 'Epicure' like 'Superb' is a pippin cross, the former similar to a Cox's in appearance and flavour. Superb matures a little later than Epicure. It is slightly conical in shape, and yellowish with red streaks. The flesh is juicy and sweet.

Blenheim Orange. Season November and December. This apple is seldom grown commercially as the tree bears little fruit until fully matured. It is, however, especially famous for its excellence as both a dessert apple and a cooker. The fruit is large and round with a dull yellow skin, a red flush, and deep red streaks. The flesh is yellow, crisp, and nutty-flavoured.

Other varieties of eating apples such as Newton Pippin, Granny Smith, Golden Delicious, etc. seen frequently in the shops are generally imported from the Commonwealth and Europe.

COOKERS

Bramley's Seedling. Season November to April. Perhaps the most widely known and best cooking apple. Medium to large in size, greenish-yellow in colour with a deep set. Cooks to a fluffy pulp with a sharp, pleasant flavour.

Lane's Prince Albert. Season November to April. A shining bright green apple with white, juicy flesh. The best cooker next to Bramley's.

Apple Charlotte. See CHARLOTTE.

Apricot. Small golden fruit with a plush-like skin. This is difficult to remove unless the fruit is very ripe, and is generally done when the fruit is cooked. Apricots lend themselves to compotes, flans, and tarts, as well as bottling and drying. The normal season is mid-summer. They are imported into England in large quantities from Spain and South Africa. They may be eaten as a dessert fruit but are best cooked, when they have a delicious flavour.

Armagnac. See BRANDY.

Arrowroot. A particularly fine starch derived from the rhizomes of maranta, cultivated chiefly in the Caribbean Islands. Used for thickening fruit juice or gravies, and as a food with milk for children or invalids.

Artichoke. There are two distinct types of artichoke, Globe (*Cynara scolymus*) and Jerusalem (*Helianthus tuberosus*).

Globe artichokes are a summer vegetable, though they may be imported at other times of the year. They are the buds of a handsome perennial plant of the thistle family, and are usually served plainly boiled, hot with melted butter or cold with an oil and vinegar dressing.

The *Jerusalem artichoke* is of the sunflower family (Jerusalem is a corruption of *girasole*, Italian for sunflower), and also a perennial. The fleshy, white tubers, which have a delicate flavour, are eaten as a winter vegetable. After being peeled they may be roasted or served in various sauces.

Asbestos Mat. A round or square piece of asbestos to be placed over a gas flame to ensure slow simmering. Now that many gas cookers are fitted with special slow jets asbestos mats are unnecessary. They should not be used on electric hot-plates.

Asparagus. A delicious vegetable in season in England in late May and June. Grown in specially prepared beds, the asparagus shoots up in slender green spikes which are cut off close to the ground and tied in bundles, for the market or in the kitchen for cooking. The asparagus imported earlier in the season from Belgium and France is a different variety from that grown in England. The stems are thick, white, and tender, with the tips only showing green. Asparagus is best served as a separate course with melted butter or hollandaise sauce.

Aspic. A clear savoury jelly made from fish, chicken, or meat stock according to the dish for which it is used, e.g. salmon in aspic, *chaudfroid* of chicken, or glazing meat or game. Aspic may be slightly acidulated but as a rule the wine used in clarifying is sufficient without the addition of vinegar. Vinegar is often used to excess with the result that aspic is disliked.

Attelette (or Hâtelet). Ornamental skewers used principally for decorating glazed hams, poultry, galantines, whole fish, and so on in cold table work for banquets or other formal occasions. Attelettes were made of silver or electroplate in various sizes, the tops carrying a design of some kind, for example a sword handle, dolphin, or heraldic device. They were further ornamented with a garnish appropriate to the dish, a design of prawns, truffles, mushrooms, shapes of aspic jelly, and so on, transfixed on to the skewer before it was inserted into the joint or dish.

Atterau. Atteraux are seldom seen nowadays, which is a pity as they make an excellent hot *hors-d'œuvre* or savoury. Atteraux are small skewers filled with a variety of savoury 'titbits' – small squares of ham, cooked chicken, liver, mushrooms, shellfish, etc. – which are then coated with a thick *béchamel* sauce bound with a little egg, or left plain. The whole is dipped in beaten egg and rolled in breadcrumbs before being fried in deep fat and served piping hot.

Au Bain-Marie. This description of a dish implies that it has been cooked in a BAIN-MARIE, as distinct from being kept warm in it.

Aubergine (Eggplant). A handsome purple vegetable which lends itself to cooking in a variety of ways. Normally the season is late August to early October, but now it is prolonged in England because of imports from other countries. Aubergines, like peppers, need sun and warmth to grow and mature, and come now mostly from Spain, France, and Israel. They are especially popular in India, the country of their origin.

Au Blanc. See BLANC.

Au Bleu. See BLEU.

Au Gratin. See GRATIN.

Aurore. A name given to a soup or sauce served with white meat, eggs, or vegetables. The base is a *béchamel* sauce to which a little fresh, well-reduced tomato pulp is added.

Avgolémono. A Greek soup made from chicken stock, thickened with beaten eggs and a little rice previously boiled in the stock. It is flavoured with lemon juice.

Avocado Pear. This is a vegetable rather than a fruit, but is so called as the size and shape resemble those of a pear. Rich, dark green in colour with paler green flesh, and bland in flavour, avocados are a popular first-course dish or salad. They grow freely in a warm climate and are imported into England from various parts of the world. They are most plentiful from May to September, though obtainable all the year round.

Baba. A small cake of a light yeast mixture soaked in syrup after baking. The mixture is that of a SAVARIN, but with a small proportion of currants added, and it is baked in a dariole MOULD. Babas are sprinkled with rum before being served (*babas au rhum*).

Baclava. A sweet cake from the Middle East. Wafer-thin layers of pastry are brushed with melted butter, filled with a sandwich of chopped nuts, and then cut into squares or diamonds. After baking a boiling syrup or honey is poured over the pastries which are then left to cool.

Bacon. The cured flesh of a pig's side (FLITCH) (the cured fore and hind quarters are classified as GAMMON and HAMS respectively). The various cuts are collar (neck), streaky (flank), back (loin), and long back. Bacon can be smoked, or unsmoked (green bacon). As the latter contains little saltpetre it is particularly suitable in cooked dishes.

Bain-Marie. At one time special *bain-marie* sets were made for use in big kitchens. The set consisted of a large tin similar to a roasting tin (with handles at each end and straight sides, and which was filled with hot water), holding a number of pans, tall, narrow and with lids. A *bain-marie* is primarily intended for keeping sauces hot. See also AU BAIN-MARIE.

Bakewell Tart. An open tart of short-crust pastry, the bottom of which is lined with red jam. It is filled, with an almond cake mixture, before being baked.

Baking. A method of cooking in the oven only. Bread and cakes are the best examples of foods cooked by this method. See ROASTING.

Baking-Powder. A raising agent: a mixture of one part cream of tartar and two parts bicarbonate of soda is added to rice flour or potato starch, and the resulting powder used to make cakes rise.

Baklava. See BACLAVA.

Ballotine. A small bird or the leg of a chicken (or other bird) boned and stuffed. After cooking it may be coated with a Madeira sauce and garnished, or served cold, coated with a *chaudfroid*, decorated, and glazed with aspic. According to their size they are served whole or cut into thick slices.

Balm (*Melissa officinalis*). A perennial plant with aromatic foliage smelling of lemon (it is also known as lemon balm). Balm is a garden plant rather than one for use in the kitchen. A large handful of the leaves, fresh or dried, infused in boiling water make a refreshing 'tea'. See TISANE.

Bamboo Shoots. These are seen only in tins in England. Yellowish-white in colour, they have a delicate flavour and are good for use in curry and Chinese dishes.

Banana. The true banana is a smaller fruit than the plantain. The banana should be eaten very ripe, when the flesh is soft and juicy and full of flavour. Bananas are usually eaten raw but are good baked in the skin, or peeled and fried in butter for serving with meat or as a sweet. See PLANTAIN.

Banbury Cake. A small oval cake, originating from the town of Banbury in Oxfordshire, with an outer layer of flaky pastry filled with a rich mincemeat. See ECCLES CAKE.

Bannock (Scots). A flat cake of bread flour (wheat, oat, or barley). The raising agent may be yeast or sour milk, and baking soda and cream of tartar. The well-known Selkirk bannock is made of yeast dough, well fruited with currants, sultanas, and candied peel.

Barbecue. An outdoor meal where an animal (originally an ox) is roasted whole; derived from the French *barbe à queue*. Recently small barbecues have become popular, and special sets with a gridiron are sold for grilling chops, steaks, etc. in the garden or at a picnic.

Barcelona. A small round HAZELNUT kernel.

Barding. Laying a piece of larding bacon or pork fat over the breast of game birds deficient in fat, e.g. pheasant, or to cover small joints of lean meat, such as veal or fillet of beef, before roasting. See also LARDING.

Barley. A grain used mostly whole in the kitchen, as an addition to soups, a pudding, or a pilaff. *Pearl barley* is the grain with the husk removed. *Barley water* is an infusion of the grain, usually flavoured with lemon. Barley is also used extensively for malting.

Barm. See YEAST.

Baron of Beef. A double sirloin, i.e. one joined together at the back-bone. At one time served traditionally at City banquets.

Barquette. A small case of pastry in the form of a boat.

Basil. Sweet basil (*Ocimum basilicum*), a well-known culinary herb with a pungent, slightly peppery flavour. Particularly good with tomatoes. Widely used in Italy and France.

Bass. A round salt-water fish, silver in colour, caught off the southern coasts of England. The flesh is white and firm and the flavour good. Bass averages from 3 to 6 lb. in weight. It is not often seen on the fishmonger's slab, being mostly fished for sport.

Basting. A process carried out during the roasting of meat to keep the joint moist and succulent: the hot dripping in the tin is taken up and spooned over the meat at 15–20 minute intervals during the roasting time.

Bâtarde. See BLANCHE.

Bath Bun. Large bun, originating in Bath, made of a rich dough with a small proportion of sultanas and candied peel. The characteristic of a bath bun is coarse sugar crystals sprinkled over the top.

Bath Chap. Pig's cheek, cured and smoked. They are frequently sold ready cooked but if not they are boiled and finished in the same way as ham.

Batter. A mixture of flour, eggs, and milk. The proportions vary according to the use to which the batter is to be put, e.g. a thick batter for Yorkshire pudding and a thin one for pancakes.

Batterie de Cuisine. French term for cooking utensils, pots, pans, etc., necessary to equip a kitchen.

Bavarois. A rich custard of egg-yolks, milk, and cream, set with gelatine, and with various flavours – vanilla, coffee, chocolate, etc.

Bay. The aromatic leaves of the bay tree (*Laurus nobilis*) are used to flavour soups, meat dishes, sauces, etc. One of the three herbs which compose a BOUQUET GARNI.

Bean. Two varieties of bean are cultivated in England, the broad bean (*Vicia faba*), and the kidney bean (*Phaseolus*); french and runner beans are members of the latter family. Many kinds of these beans are grown, some for use as a green vegetable, and others more suited for drying, e.g. haricot and butter beans.

Broad bean. In season from early June until the end of July. The beans, grey-green in colour, are bedded in a soft, white, fibrous material in long green pods. Like most summer vegetables, broad beans should be eaten when young and small. If, however, the beans are large the outer grey coat must be peeled off after cooking. Broad beans are the classic accompaniment to boiled bacon and may be either tossed with butter and chopped savory, or mixed with a *poulette* sauce.

French bean. A dwarf bean with long, smooth, green pods about 4–5 inches long. The pods are eaten when young, whole or snapped in

half. In season from mid-June to the end of July. See also FLAGEO-
LET, below.

Runner bean. Sometimes called 'stick' bean, as it is grown up poles
or sticks. The plant reaches 7–8 feet in height, though varieties are
now grown 3–4 feet high with a proportionately smaller pod. This is a
bright dark green with a rougher exterior than a french bean. The
pods can reach 8–10 inches in length and still be juicy and tender.
They are sliced for boiling. In shops 'stick' beans fetch a better price
than the field runner, as they are cleaner and of better quality. Season
from early July to the middle or end of August.

Flageolet, or Lima, bean. A type of small haricot bean. These are the
beans which lie inside the pod of a variety of french bean and are sold
fresh or dried after the outer jacket has been removed. Pale green in
colour, they have a good flavour and are something of a delicacy.

Haricot bean. A small white bean, dried, and used largely for canning,
in soups and stews, and as a vegetable. Coloured varieties of the haricot bean are also sold, mostly in Continental shops, such as the
Brown Dutch bean and the red *Rognon de Coq.*

Butter bean. A large white bean, also dried, used mostly as a vegetable.

Béarnaise. One of the rich butter sauces. Made like HOLLAN-
DAISE, but sharper in taste and thicker in consistency. Finished
with chopped tarragon and chervil. Served with roast fillet of
beef, tournedos, and steaks.

Béchamel. A white sauce. One of the *sauces mères* from which
other sauces are derived. The sauce is thickened with a *roux* of
butter and flour, and the milk is infused with an onion, a bay
leaf, a blade of mace, and peppercorns, to flavour it, before
being added to the *roux.*

Beef. The meat of a young ox or bullock. Prime quality beef can
be English or Scotch and is specially bred for flavour and size.
Nowadays this is of importance, as small compact joints are the
most popular. The diagram of a side of beef overleaf shows the
division into joints.

Beer. A fermented liquor made from malted barley flavoured
with hops.

15

Beef

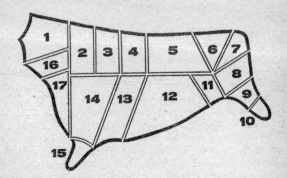

1. Neck – *Stew*.
2. Chuck ribs – *Braise*.
3. Middle ribs – *Braise*.
4. Fore ribs – *Roast*.
5. Sirloin – *Roast or grill as steaks*.
6. Rump – *Grill*.
7. Aitchbone – *Roast or braise*.
8. Topside and silverside – *Roast or braise*.
9. Buttock and silverside – *boil, salted or fresh*.
10. Shin and cow heel – *Stew*.
11. Thick flank – *Stew, boil, braise, or press*.
12. Thin flank – *As Thick flank*.
13. Brisket – *Boil, plain or salted – can be pressed*.
14. Leg of mutton piece (Chuck steak) – *Braise or stew*.
15. Shin – *Gravy beef, stew, beef tea*.
16. Sticking piece – *Stew*.
17. Clod – *Stew*.

Beestings. The first milking after a cow has calved. The rich milk is used to make a baked custard which sets without eggs.

Beetroot. A well-known winter root vegetable, rich dark red in colour. The root may be round (globe) or tapered. Beetroots should be well washed before being boiled in their skins (if cut or pricked before cooking they will 'bleed' and lose their colour). After boiling the skins are rubbed off; when they are easy to remove the beetroot is cooked. Other varieties of beet-

16

root, cultivated for their stems and foliage, are sea-kale beet (see CHARD) and spinach beet (see SPINACH).

Beignet. French for fritter, e.g. *beignets de pommes*, apple fritters. *Beignets* are also small spoonfuls of chou pastry dropped into very hot deep fat. The temperature is gradually raised as they fry, allowing them to puff well and turn a golden-brown. After being drained, the *beignets* are rolled in caster sugar and served hot with a jam sauce, or rolled in grated Parmesan for serving as a savoury.

Benedictine. An old French liqueur invented and made from a secret formula by the Benedictine monks at Fécamp.

Benedictine and Brandy. A mixture of Benedictine and brandy now sold in bottles.

Bercy. A sauce made of white wine, light stock, shallots, and chopped herbs. The food (fish, veal, sweetbreads, etc.) may be cooked in these ingredients, or poached in stock which is then strained into the white wine, etc. The sauce is lightly thickened with BEURRE MANIÉ.

Beurre Blanc (French for white butter). A sauce served with boiled or poached white fish. Good unsalted butter is added by degrees to well-reduced white wine and chopped shallot over very gentle heat. The consistency and colour are those of smooth cream.

Beurre Manié. Butter and flour worked together to a paste. The proportions are 1½ parts of butter to 1 of flour. This liaison is added to the liquid in which food has been poached or simmered. The liquid must be well off the boil before the *beurre manié* is added in small pieces. Once the butter has melted and drawn the flour into the liquid, the whole is re-boiled.

Beurre Noir (French for black butter). Butter which is cooked to a deep nut-brown and acidulated with reduced vinegar, chopped capers, and parsley. *Beurre noir* is poured over fish, sweetbreads, brains, etc. which have been poached in a COURT-BOUILLON; e.g. *cervelles au beurre noir, raie au beurre noir*, etc.

17

Beurre Noisette. Butter cooked to a nut-brown (usually in a frying pan). A good squeeze of lemon juice is added with chopped parsley and seasoning, and the whole poured foaming over the dish, e.g. *sole meunière*, just before serving.

Bicarbonate of Soda. See SODA.

Bigarade. French for a Seville orange. Bigarade sauce usually accompanies duck or game. It has a *demi-glace* base to which red wine, red-currant jelly, the juice of the orange, and a little of the blanched shredded rind are added.

Bigarreau. See CHERRY.

Bilberry. The fruit of a low-growing wild moorland or heath plant (*Vaccinium myrtillus*). The name varies in different parts of England, whortleberry, blaeberry, hurt, etc. The fruit is small and black, with a pleasant though not exciting flavour, and may be gathered from late June to the end of July. Bilberries can be stewed or made into wine.

Biscotins. French for small biscuits of various kinds served with cream sweets, ices, etc. They are sold in England in packets.

Biscotte. Similar to a rusk or to English 'pulled' bread: slices or small pieces of milk bread, baked to a light golden-brown. They are sold in packets in England.

Biscuit. A type of unleavened bread. Most countries have their own kinds of biscuit, but perhaps Great Britain excels in the variety of commercially made biscuits – plain, sweet, and savoury. Most biscuits are rolled thinly and cut into rounds and well pricked before being baked. A biscuit pricker, a round 'pin-cushion' filled with short spikes, is sold for this purpose. 'Fancy' biscuits, cut into different shapes, have sugared tops or are sandwiched with a flavoured cream.

Bisque. A rich soup made from shellfish, e.g. lobster bisque, prawn bisque. The base of the soup is the *court-bouillon* with white wine in which the fish was cooked. After being strained the bisque is thickened with a *roux* and finished with cream and a flavoured butter made from the pounded shellfish. See also VELOUTÉ.

Blackberry (*Rubus fruticosus*). A popular wild fruit coming into season in September. Garden or cultivated blackberries are also grown. Blackberries contain little pectin so apple is used to set jam and jelly. Because of their seeds blackberries are usually puréed after cooking and used to make fool or a sauce.

Blackcock or **Black Game.** In season from 20 August to 10 December. A species of grouse, blackcock is a handsome bird with shining blue-black plumage distinguished by white bars above the wing-tips. The cock weighs anything from 3 to 4 lb.; the hen is much smaller, with reddish-brown plumage. Black-cock is fairly uncommon, though now increasing especially in Scotland. The flesh is very like that of grouse, and it is cooked in the same way.

Black-currant. A summer fruit rich in pectin and vitamin C. In season from late June to the end of July. Like blackberries, black-currants are best puréed for use in sauces, fool, and soufflés. See also CURRANT.

Black Pudding. A large sausage, black in colour, sometimes seen with the ends tied together to form a circle. There are various recipes for making black pudding but in the main the ingredients are finely minced trimmings of pork fat, onions, herbs, and pig's blood. A filling of oatmeal or bread can also be used. The mixture is put into the prepared gut and tied up, and the puddings are boiled. Once cooked they may be kept for several days. They may be re-boiled for serving hot, or cut into slices and fried. See WHITE PUDDING.

Blaeberry. See BILBERRY.

Blanc (French for white). In cooking terms *au blanc* means that a dish is kept white by cooking, and served with a white or cream sauce.

Blanch. Literally to whiten, but the term can also be applied to green vegetables, which are not made white in the process. It is

19

generally done to remove any strong and possibly disagreeable taste. White meats and root vegetables are put into cold water and brought to the boil before being drained and cooked further. Green vegetables or those where it is important to keep the colour are put into boiling water and boiled for the specified time before being drained.

Blanche. A white sauce made with a *roux* on to which boiling water is poured. The sauce must not be boiled once this has been done, but more butter added as with hollandaise. *Sauce blanche* is served with vegetables, fish, or chicken and also forms the base of mustard sauce, caper sauce, and green sauce.

Sauce bâtarde (mock hollandaise) is made in the same way but with the addition of 1 or 2 egg-yolks.

Blancmange. A corruption of *blanc-manger*, 'something white to eat'. Originally a blancmange was a kind of almond cream, but now is an old-fashioned word for a cornflour 'shape' or mould.

Blanquette. Corresponding to a fricassée, but with the sauce made from the liquor in which the meat – veal, chicken or rabbit – has been cooked. The sauce is finished with a little rich milk or cream, and sometimes has a liaison of egg-yolks.

Blette. See CHARD.

Bleu (Au Bleu). A method of cooking trout. The fish must be freshly killed and is put into an acidulated *court-bouillon* to poach. When cooked the skin has a bluish tinge. The trout are served with boiled potatoes and melted butter.

Blewit. One of the best-known of edible fungi, belonging to the genus *Tricholoma*. Blewits are firm-fleshed, with a pleasant smell and delicate flavour. There are two varieties: *Tricholoma nudum*, the wood blewit, violet in colour and growing in oak woods in autumn; and *Tricholoma personaltum*, the blewit with a fawn cap and violet-tinged stem and gills. Both fungi can be cooked in the same way as mushrooms.

Blini. A thick pancake made with buckwheat or plain flour and raised with yeast. Blinis are the traditional Russian accompaniment to caviar and are served hot, layered with sour cream or melted butter.

Bloater. A herring that has been salted in brine, strung through the gills on thin wooden rods to dry, then lightly smoked. Bloaters are left whole, and for cooking are best grilled. They are a speciality of Great Yarmouth.

Boil. To cook foods in water or stock. The boiling-point of water is 212° F., and at this stage it should bubble. To ensure this, allow the liquid to boil for a minute or two before leaving the pan to cook, as the water will often move before boiling-point is actually reached. A 'rolling' boil is one where the water boils very fast. Few ingredients in cookery should boil quickly; more often SIMMERING is called for.

Bombe. See MOULD.

Bonne Femme. The name given to a dish of meat or chicken, usually cooked *en casserole*, and garnished with small onions, bacon, and mushrooms. Fillets of sole *bonne femme* are served with a white wine sauce with mushrooms, the whole glazed under the grill.

Borage. A herb (*Borago officinalis*) a spray or two of which is used to flavour a wine or fruit cup. It has a distinct cucumber flavour and is slightly aromatic.

Bordeaux. A term usually applied to the wines, both red and white, produced in the region of Bordeaux. Red Bordeaux is known as claret in England. Bordeaux wines are easily distinguished by the shape of the bottle: it has a high shoulder near the neck as opposed to the sloping neck of, for example, a Burgundy bottle.

Bordelais. Literally, of Bordeaux. A dish cooked *à la bordelaise* has been cooked with red wine. *Sauce bordelaise* is a red wine sauce with pieces of beef marrow in it.

Border. See MOULD.

21

Borshch. A Russian and Polish soup made of strong beef stock well flavoured with beetroot, and finished with sour cream. Borshch may be clear, i.e. a CONSOMMÉ, or thick with vegetables.

Bouchée (French for a mouthful). A small case of puff pastry filled with a savoury mixture, e.g. cooked chicken shredded and bound with a *velouté* sauce.

Bouillabaisse. A soup or broth made of several different kinds of fish stewed gently together until the consistency is almost that of a stew. *Bouillabaisse* is a speciality of the French Mediterranean coast. The vegetables and spices (particularly saffron) added vary according to the district.

Bouillon. French for stock (meat or vegetable).

Boulangère, à la. Baked in the oven. From the French *boulanger* (baker). A century and more ago the local baker's oven was used by housewives to cook joints or pies. Today *à la boulangère* means potatoes and onions cooked in stock with the meat, or separately.

Bouquet Garni. French for faggot. The traditional ingredients are parsley, thyme, and a bay leaf. They are tied together and added to a stew, casserole, or sauce for flavouring.

Bourguignonne. Literally, of Burgundy or from that region. *À la bourguignonne* means cooked with red wine, mushrooms, and onions.

Brains. Classed as offal. Those eaten are from a calf or sheep.

Braising. A method of cooking by moist heat (as opposed to roasting) especially suited to cuts of meat that call for long, slow cooking. After being browned the meat is placed on a bed of vegetables with a small quantity of liquid, then the pan or pot is tightly covered and put into the oven. This ensures all-over heat. Braising pans or pots were once made with a concave lid, so that hot water could be put on top with the same object in view.

Bran. The inner husk of wheat and other grains. Bran is removed in milling white wheat flour, but is present in brown or wholemeal flour. It is a valuable form of roughage.

Brandade. A rich 'cream' of fish, made by working cooked salt cod (French *morue*) with warm olive oil and sometimes milk over gentle heat. Garlic is added to flavour. When it has become a soft rich mass, the *brandade* is served hot with crisp *croûtes* of fried bread. *Brandade* is also served cold as part of a *hors-d'œuvre* or as a first course.

Brandy. A spirit distilled from wine. The finest is cognac made from white wines grown in the Charente district of France. When it is first distilled brandy is colourless but after maturing in the cask it takes colour from the wood. Some manufacturers add artificial colouring. A type of brandy can also be distilled from wine and indeed from grain alcohol. *Armagnac* is also a brandy, made from wines grown in that district (south-west France). See also EAU-DE-VIE.

Brandy Snap. Also called Ginger Snap. A crisp wafer-like biscuit rolled when baked into a cornet or cylinder. The ingredients are flour, butter, syrup, sugar, and ginger to flavour. The centre may be filled with whipped cream, and this may be flavoured with brandy.

Brawn. A dish for the cold table made from a pig's head gently stewed until very tender. All the meat, including the tongue, is picked off the bones, roughly chopped, and put into a special press or brawn mould. Alternatively the meat is turned into small basins and pressed into shape by a weight. When cold the brawn is turned out and sliced thinly for serving, either plain or with a sharp dressing.

Brazil Nut. The seed of a tall handsome tree (*Bertholletia excelsa*) found particularly on the banks of the Orinoco and in the northern parts of Brazil. Up to thirty-two seeds or nuts are contained in one round fruit in four divisions, which accounts for the triangular shape of the seeds. Each has an exceptionally hard shell and a pure white kernel which is very rich in oil. The kernels are seldom used in cooking but are popular as a dessert, particularly at Christmas.

Bread. Bread can be divided into three main classes: (1) The flour is made into a paste or dough with water or milk, and raised or leavened by yeast. (2) As above, but the raising agent is either baking-powder or bicarbonate of soda and cream of tartar. Here the liquid should be milk, preferably sour milk or butter milk, for lightness. This bread is known as baking-powder bread or soda bread and is baked in large rounds cut into four (farls) either in the oven or on a girdle. The dough is also suitable for making into scones. (3) Unleavened bread, such as water biscuits, oatcakes, etc. Bread made with yeast and water has a crisp crust; that mixed with milk is very white and soft in texture with a soft crust owing to the presence of fat. Some breads, especially Continental ones, have a comparatively high proportion of yeast to flour which gives an open spongy texture, as does a slack dough. A low proportion of yeast, say 1 oz. to 4–5 lb. flour, will give a close-textured bread, and so does a drier, firmer dough. French bread is made and baked in a slightly different way from English household bread: steam is introduced into the oven while the loaves are baking. See also BRAN, FLOUR, GLUTEN, and YEAST.

Bread Sauce. The most famous and according to one authority the only sauce that England has produced. Badly made it is a bread poultice; but light and creamy, it is a perfect accompaniment to roast chicken or baked or boiled ham. Fresh white breadcrumbs are added to milk flavoured with a whole onion stuck with a clove. The sauce should only just be allowed to boil so that it thickens. It is then finished with a knob of butter or a spoonful of cream.

Bream. There are two varieties of bream, fresh-water or carp bream, and salt-water or sea bream. The fresh-water bream is poor and inclined to be muddy in flavour, as it lives in large ponds and slow-running rivers. The sea bream has a pink tinge to the skin, which is covered with large tough scales. The flesh is coarse-textured, and the flavour again is dull. Bream is best stuffed and baked, or served poached, whole or filleted, with a piquant sauce. Both kinds of bream are round fish, small to medium in size.

Bretonne, à la. (a) The name given to a dish of roast or braised mutton accompanied by haricot beans cooked separately, sometimes as a purée. (b) *Sauce bretonne* consists of shredded root vegetables – carrot, onion, celery and leek – cooked in butter and added to a thick *velouté* sauce. It is served with fish, or poached or soft-boiled eggs.

Brie. A soft creamy cheese, melting when ripe, first made at La Brie near Paris. The cheese is large, round, and flat, not more than about an inch thick, and with a creamy white crust resembling that of a Camembert. At the point of perfection the texture and flavour of Brie are excellent. When buying Brie, have it cut from the whole cheese, so that you can judge its state of ripeness. Unfortunately Brie, like Camembert, is too often sold cut, wrapped, and boxed in small sections.

Brill. A medium-sized flat fish, brown on top and creamy white on the underside. The flesh somewhat resembles that of turbot, though it is not so firm. Brill is at its best from September to May and can be cooked whole or filletted in the same way as sole or turbot.

Brine. A strong solution of salt and water used for salting or pickling meats, etc.

Brioche. A very light yeast dough or paste shaped like a miniature cottage loaf and baked in a small fluted mould. Brioches are made small, medium-sized, or large for slicing like a loaf. When baked, they should be a rich nut-brown. Brioche paste can also be fried in small pieces in deep fat like the English doughnut.

Brisling. The young of herring. Mostly found tinned in England. See also SPRAT.

Broccoli (*Oleracea asparagoides*). Very like CAULIFLOWER, but larger and with less compact flowers. It does not have as delicate a flavour as cauliflower. Broccoli are in season in early to late spring. Purple-sprouting broccoli flowers at the end of March and has small purple heads resembling the white broccoli, but several growing on the same plant. Once it has been cut more will form. It is delicious served plainly boiled with melted butter or hollandaise sauce. The small spears may be eaten like asparagus.

Broche, à la or en. Cooked or roasted on a spit ('spit' is *broche*). Mechanical spits, either gas or electric, are sold for cooking chickens, small birds, and joints *en broche*.

Brochette. A small skewer of wood or metal on which pieces of meat, etc. are skewered for grilling. See KABAB.

Broiler. See CHICKEN.

Broiling. See GRILLING.

Brown Sauce. A fine MIREPOIX is cooked in butter, then flour is added to form a *roux*. Stock is added and the sauce finished as for a DEMI-GLACE. Butter helps to improve the colour of the sauce, if the stock is not of the first quality.

Brunoise. A very fine dice or MIREPOIX of vegetables cooked in a nut of butter. Used as a garnish for soups, etc.

Brussels Sprout. A member of the *Brassica* family. Sprouts are essentially a winter vegetable and for perfection should be picked and eaten when they are small and tight. They are considered to be at their best after the first frosts.

Bubble and Squeak (A *réchauffé*). Slices of cooked beef, fried and arranged round boiled chopped cabbage which is also fried.

Buckling. Herrings that are smoked whole. Bucklings are eaten as a first course with an onion salad and sliced dill cucumbers. They need no further cooking.

Buckwheat. The seed of *Fagopyrum esculentum*. Buckwheat is not very well known in England, but ground into a meal or flour it is popular made into pancakes or crumpets in the United States. Buckwheat is also the flour used in making BLINIS.

Buffet. A long table or sideboard on which are laid various cold fish, chicken, salad, and meat dishes, as well as cold sweets. Plates, forks, etc. may be arranged on the front of the table for the guests to help themselves, or they may be served from the buffet. Hot dishes can also be on the buffet depending on the occasion. Dishes for a buffet should be chosen with an eye to colour and variety.

Bullace. A small, greenish-yellow, rather sour plum about the size of a sloe. Bullaces are not often seen nowadays except in country districts. They make excellent jam or fruit cheese.

Bun. A name for small pieces of a light yeast dough either plain or enriched with dried fruit, and shaped into balls. After they have been proved and baked, the tops are sugared or glazed before they come out of the oven. There are several varieties of buns, the best known being hot cross buns, traditional on Good Friday, Bath buns, Chelsea buns, etc.

Burgundy. Red and white wines, largely the produce of the Côte d'Or though Upper and Lower Burgundy have a considerable output too. Beaune is the centre of the wine trade in this area.

Butter. Butter is the finest fat for use in the kitchen. It is produced by churning ripened cream in special temperature conditions. The fat globules from milk, and thence cream, are broken down by the movement of churning and so massed into butter. *Buttermilk* is a by-product of this process and is the liquid which remains after the butter has 'come', or solidified. Buttermilk is a wholesome drink, with a pleasant sharp taste from the acidity developed in ripening the cream. It is ideal for making scones and soda bread. Butter may be fresh (unsalted) or salted. Ideally butter should be unsalted for cooking purposes: it is better for frying and has the maximum of flavour for adding to vegetables. *Clarified butter* is butter which is heated and strained to separate any liquid, such as buttermilk, etc., from it. This ensures that it will keep and makes it ideal for frying. See CLARIFY.

Butter Cream. A soft rich mixture used for filling, coating, and decorating *gâteaux* and *pâtisserie* generally. There are three types: (1) with a yolk and syrup base; (2) with a *meringue cuite* base (see MERINGUE); (3) with a custard base. To each of these mixtures is added well-creamed, unsalted butter. Butter cream may be flavoured with coffee, chocolate, orange, etc., or a fresh fruit purée, such as strawberry or raspberry.

Butter Icing. See ICING.

Buttermilk. See BUTTER.

Cabbage. One of the best-known vegetables belonging to the *Brassica* family, which also includes sprouts, cauliflower, broccoli, and kale. What is not generally appreciated is that there are several varieties of cabbage which are more suited to certain dishes than to others, and which also are in season at different times of the year.

SPRING CABBAGE

In season from May to the end of July, easily recognized by its oval, pointed heart of a delicate brilliant green. The outer leaves fan out from the heart and are of a darker, almost bluish, green. The cabbage is not large, and as it is ready early in the year every leaf is tender. To get the full flavour spring cabbage is best just quartered, plainly boiled, and finished in butter well sprinkled with chopped parsley or herbs.

WINTER CABBAGES

After September the winter cabbages come into their own, and of these there are several types.

Green Cabbage. This is an all-purpose cabbage of moderate size (around 2 lb. in weight), with a round, firm heart, at its best from late September to February. There are different varieties, some early, some late, to ensure a good sequence.

Drum-head or White Dutch. A large, white, hard-hearted variety, principally used shredded in salads, or cooked in butter with a very little wine or stock, i.e. *à l'alsacienne*.

Savoy Cabbage. This is bright green in colour with very crinkled leaves, and is in season from December onwards. It takes little harm from severe frost, and, though the outside leaves may become brown and rotten-looking, the heart remains crisp and sweet. Savoys are especially good braised and served with rolled bacon, or boiled whole and covered with a white sauce.

Red Cabbage. One that calls for longer cooking or stewing than the Drum-head. It is best shredded finely before cooking, and should be blanched in boiling water. After it has been drained, a good deal of the colour will have been lost, but is restored by the addition of 1–2 tablespoons of vinegar, sprinkled over the cabbage together with a little sugar and salt. After being moistened with about ½ gill stock the pan is tightly covered and the whole cooked slowly for 1–2 hours or until tender. Red cabbage is served with rich meats such as pork, hare, and game of all kinds. Apple is sometimes cooked with it. It is also excellent as a salad and makes a good winter pickle.

Cabbage Lettuce. See LETTUCE.

Cabinet Pudding. A hot pudding, not often met with today. Breadcrumbs baked in a custard with currants form the base; it may be flavoured with lemon rind or vanilla.

Caerphilly. Originally a Welsh cheese but now made in the western counties. White in colour and mild in flavour with a close firm texture. It should be eaten when freshly bought.

Cake. A name which covers a wide variety of the familiar objects which appear on our tea-tables, and, in these days, frequently as a pudding for lunch or dinner. Basically cakes are a composition of fat, sugar, eggs, and flour. They may be enriched with dried fruit or flavoured with chocolate, coffee, orange, and so on.

Calabresse. Closely resembles a deep-cream-coloured sprouting BROCCOLI with a greenish tinge. It is in season in late summer.

Calf. See VEAL.

Camembert. The most famous of French cheeses, first made by a farmer's wife in the little village of Camembert. It weighs about 12 oz. and is packed in round chip boxes. It is a soft cheese, but must not be runny. The texture is smooth, and it is pale yellow in colour, with a yellowish-orange crust.

Camomile (or **Chamomile**). The dried flower heads of *Anthemis nobilis* used as an infusion (see TISANE).

Canapé. A small round of fried or toasted bread, pastry or savoury biscuit spread or piled up with a savoury mixture and served hot or cold. Like all savouries it should appeal to the eye as well as to the palate. See CROÛTE.

Candied Peel. The rind or peel of citrus fruits, the most usual being orange, lemon, and citron. It is used principally with dried fruit for cakes and puddings, or at times as a sweetmeat. As a rule it is commercially prepared, though a good substitute can be made at home. Sound fruit is cut in half and the pulp or flesh removed. The pith and peel are retained and boiled gently in water until tender. They are then well drained, and immersed in a strong syrup until they become semi-transparent. After further draining they are dried in gentle heat. To quicken the process of candying the rinds may be simmered gently in the syrup until translucent. In this case the syrup should be thinner (i.e. well below the thread – see SYRUP) when the rinds are first added. During simmering the syrup reduces until thick and the rinds become semi-clear. Dry as described above.

Candy. A grained or granulated confection. To prepare it, a sugar syrup is boiled to 250° F., and graining is then induced by gentle stirring round the sides of the pan only. Once the syrup has started to cloud and thicken, stir until all is well grained, adding a chosen flavouring. Turn on to a *warmed* oiled tin or marble, and leave till cold before breaking into pieces.

Cannelloni. An Italian PASTA in the form of large tubes. These are parboiled and stuffed with a farce such as is used for *ravioli*, and the cooking is completed in stock or sauce. Alternatively, thin pancakes are used in place of the *pasta* and stuffed; they may be coated with a cream or cheese sauce.

Cape Gooseberry (*Physalis*). A round yellow berry enclosed in a calyx like a dead leaf. The edible *physalis* should not be confused with the Japanese lantern plant. Though similar in appearance, the berry of the latter is not so well formed. Cape gooseberries are canned (golden berries) or made into jam. Both are imported

into England from South Africa. Fresh cape gooseberries are
sold by the dozen around Christmas time; they can be eaten as
a dessert, or the calyx may be bent back and the berry dipped
into fondant and eaten as a sweetmeat.

Caper. Capers are the buds of *Capparis spinosa*, a handsome
plant cultivated in France, Italy, and Spain. The smaller the
caper the more delicate the flavour, and so the buds are graded
before being bottled. The grades are named, the nonpareils and
capuchins being the finest. Capers are used principally for
flavouring sauces, e.g. caper sauce with mutton, or tartare sauce,
and for garnishing. Imitation capers can be produced by pickling nasturtium seeds in vinegar. These are usually first salted
in brine.

Capercailzie. A large game bird which was quite common in
Scotland but is now scarce. The average weight is 10–12 lb., and
the flesh is somewhat like that of grouse. It may be stuffed and
plainly roasted.

Capon. A young cock fowl castrated by injection and specially
fattened for the table. The flesh is white and delicate, and the
weight averages around 7–8 lb. The bird may be stuffed and
roasted like a turkey. Capons are also especially suitable for the
cold table; here the bird is poached and the suprême removed
and sliced. The breast-bone is cut away and the carcass filled
with a mousse of ham or *foie gras*, etc. The slices are replaced to
re-form the bird and the whole is coated with a *chaudfroid* sauce,
decorated and glazed with aspic. Alternatively, aspic jelly only
may be used, in which case the bird is best roasted. A *poularde* is
the hen bird, and is treated in the same way.

Capsicum. Capsicum is the family name of chillies and peppers.
These vary from the red-hot chilli to the sweet pepper, the large
green or red variety known as bell peppers (sometimes called
pimentos), which are now common in the shops. Chillies are
used for chutneys and pickles and for flavouring vinegar, etc.,
while peppers find a place in salads, stews, and rice and curry
dishes. They are more digestible if shredded and blanched

before being used in a dish. Peppers are also tinned, particularly the sweet red peppers. Dried and ground, chillies become cayenne pepper or chilli powder, red pimentoes become paprika.

Caramel (or **Burnt Sugar**). This is the last but one stage in sugar boiling (see SYRUP), and one which is aromatic and piquant in flavour. Caramel is used as a flavouring, principally for sweets, though as 'Black Jack' (the last degree in sugar boiling) it is employed as a gravy browning, or as a colouring for fruit cakes. For a quick home-made browning put enough granulated sugar in an old metal spoon to half-fill it. Hold it above a gas flame and let it melt and bubble until it is almost black. Put a few drops into the gravy or sauce. Alternatively, use a small saucepan and treat the sugar in the same way. Add 2–3 tablespoons water when the sugar is burnt. This method should be used for a solid fuel stove.

Caraway. Though caraway grows wild in Britain, the plant *Carum carvi* is cultivated abroad, largely in southern Europe, for the seeds. These, pungent and aromatic, are used to flavour bread, cakes, biscuits, cheese, pickles, and so on. Caraway seeds are also made into comfits. The plant itself is feathery in leaf with flat white flower heads, and is very like cummin in both appearance and flower.

Carbonnade. The name carbonnade is derived from carbon, and means grilled or broiled over the coals. Today a carbonnade is a rich ragout or stew made with beer, and is one of the best-known Flemish dishes. Its chief characteristic is that it has a crust of bread well soaked in any fat which rises to the surface, and as the dish is cooked in the oven the bread becomes golden-brown and crisp.

Cardamom (*Amomum cardamomum*). A spice largely used in the making of curry powder, and also in medicine as a carminative. The seeds are small and black and are contained in a white outer case or capsule, usually three or four seeds to one capsule. The

B

flavour is pungent and aromatic. Like caraway, cardamoms are made into comfits.

Cardinal. A name given to dishes and sauces naturally coloured a bright red, e.g. lobster cardinal, apples cardinal (with a strawberry sauce), and so on.

Cardoon (*Cynara cardunculus*). Cardoons are not well known in England. The nearest approximation in appearance and flavour is the sea-kale beet. The cardoon is blanched while growing; the stalks grow white, crisp, and tender, and are cooked in much the same way as sea-kale.

Carmine or **Cochineal.** Cochineal, obtained from the cochineal insect, is bluish-red in colour. By further processing, a more brilliant colour known as carmine can be made.

Carp. A fresh-water fish much esteemed in Europe and in countries far from the sea. The carp family is a large one; tench, BREAM, chub, and goldfish are members of it. The culinary carp and the one stocked by fishmongers is the golden carp. Averaging 2–4 lb. in weight, with a thick, scaly skin and a golden sheen, and flesh in large white flakes, the carp lends itself to boiling and braising on a bed of vegetables, and especially to gefilte fish. In this dish, the flesh is taken out (leaving the skin whole), minced, and worked with water, onions, and herbs; when it is a mousse it is stuffed back into the skin. The whole is poached or braised, and after cooking cut into slices for serving with the cooking juices.

Carrageen. Irish sea moss. This edible seaweed, which is also known as Iberian moss, was very popular at one time and much valued as a food for invalids and children. It is gelatinous in texture and can be used in place of isinglass. Carrageen is light brown in colour when growing on the rocks. It should be thoroughly washed to remove all trace of salt, and then spread out to bleach out of doors, so that it can get further washing by rain. When a creamy white the carrageen is hung up to dry. Before use, it is soaked in water to soften. It can be gently stewed in milk for making a jelly or blancmange.

Carrot (*Dancus carota*). An indispensable vegetable. Mild and unobtrusive, it none the less plays an important role in the kitchen, from the stockpot to jam-making, and is the most tender and delectable of all spring vegetables. Not only were carrots known to the ancient Greeks, but, according to one source, in the reigns of Charles I and James I ladies were in the habit of decorating their head-dresses with the delicate and fern-like leaves. Recipes for carrots are legion, an indication that the taste of carrots, like those of potatoes and bread, does not pall.

Cashew. A kidney-shaped nut with a piquant flavour. The kernels are usually fried in butter and then salted, to be eaten as a cocktail nut. Pounded they can be added to a *velouté* sauce to serve with chicken or turkey.

Casserole. A container (usually round) of earthenware, glazed china, or metal, with a lid. Designed for long slow cooking of meat or game. By extension the word may also denote the food cooked in a casserole.

Cassis. A liqueur made from black-currant skins.

Cassolette. A thin batter case fried on a special mould in deep fat, and then filled with any good savoury mixture: scrambled eggs and cheese, shrimps, kidneys, etc.

Cassoulet. A famous French hot-pot of haricot beans and pickled goose (*confit d'oie*) from Languedoc. There are several varieties of cassoulet but the essentials are the same.

Castle Pudding. A hot pudding. A Victoria sponge mixture baked or steamed in a dariole or castle pudding MOULD and served with a jam sauce.

Caudle. Gruel of oatmeal enriched with spices and wine.

Caul. The membrane enclosing the foetus. Caul for culinary purposes is taken from the sheep or pig and when cleansed and prepared by the butcher resembles a thick veil ribbed with white fat. Caul is used to protect food from the heat of the oven and to give fat; e.g. a piece of caul is often sold with a leg of mutton to cover it while it is roasting.

Cauliflower (*Oleracea botrylis*). A delicately flavoured vegetable. To be perfect the flower should be white and close, and the leaves a soft bright green. The outside leaves are long, and as the plant grows and the flower forms the spines of a few of them are broken and bent over the flower to keep it blanched and white. In England cauliflowers are in season from summer to late autumn, after which they are imported from Italy and other European countries. When preparing either cauliflower or BROCCOLI care must be taken not to cut off all the green; three or four of the young leaves curled round the flower should be left. They add to the appearance and flavour and help to keep the flower from breaking while being cooked. Cauliflowers are first boiled gently, flower uppermost, and when served as an accompanying vegetable are coated with a *béchamel* or white sauce, or well sprinkled with white breadcrumbs fried to a golden-brown in plenty of butter. The classic dish is cauliflower cheese or *gratiné Mornay*, in which the cauliflower is coated with a rich cheese sauce, and well browned in the oven. Cauliflowers are good, too, as a salad with mayonnaise or vinaigrette dressing; or the sprigs can be coated with batter, fried, and served with a tomato or tartare sauce. See CALABRESSE.

Caviar. Comes from the roe of STURGEON. The best caviar is imported from Russia, and is an expensive luxury. The appearance is hardly attractive, a mass of small grey-black eggs the size of a large pin-head, but the flavour more than makes up for it. Caviar is served as an *hors-d'œuvre*, ice cold and accompanied by hot toast, pats of fresh butter, and quarters of lemon. Traditionally BLINIS should accompany it. Canapés of caviar are also served with champagne or cocktails.

Cayenne. Red pepper from chillies. See CAPSICUM.

Celeriac (*Apium rapaceum*). Root celery resembling a large turnip and in season from late November to the end of February. A most useful vegetable served cooked in pieces or as a purée, or raw, shredded, and blanched as a salad.

Celery (*Apium graveolens*). A popular salad vegetable but equally good cooked. English or garden celery is in season from late October to January, but imported celery is around from late June. The blanched stalk of the plant is eaten, while the root, seeds, and leaves may be used for flavouring chutneys, relishes, stews, and bottled sauces.

Cep or Cèpe (*Boletus edulis*). A fungus well known and popular in France. In England, where it also grows, it is gathered and cooked by the comparative few who not only like ceps but can recognize them. They are the size of a large mushroom with a shiny brown top and thick white stem. The cap is also thick, with a spongy type of gill. This is generally removed and the flesh cut into thick slices and fried in olive oil flavoured with garlic. Ceps are also good stewed as a ragout or fried in butter to accompany any meat dish; in fact cooked in the same ways as mushrooms.

Chafing Dish. A deep frying-pan on a spirit or butane gas lamp or electrically heated. It is used for cookery done at the table, i.e. quick dishes such as scrambled eggs, ragout of kidneys.

Chambertin. A rich, full-flavoured Burgundy. A name given to certain recipes, e.g. *poulet Chambertin*, chicken cooked in Burgundy with mushrooms.

Chamomile. See CAMOMILE.

Champagne. A sparkling white wine, so called as it is made in the district of Champagne in France. It is made sparkling by the addition of sugar at a certain stage in the development of the wine, thus producing a second fermentation. The process is a lengthy and therefore expensive one, and it takes several years before the wine becomes 'champagne'.

Chanterelle (*Cantharellus cibarius*). An edible fungus with a good, slightly peppery flavour. As popular in France as CEPS, and perhaps better known in England. Chanterelles are common in the woods in early autumn, and are easily recognizable as they resemble a golden trumpet. They are inclined to be a little tough and are best stewed slowly in rich stock.

Chantilly (*crème Chantilly*). Whipped cream lightly sweetened and flavoured with vanilla.

Chapon. A crust of bread rubbed with garlic and added to a salad to flavour it. It is used particularly with chicory. The chapon may be taken out before the salad is served.

Chapatti. An Indian bread, flat and unleavened. The paste of flour and water is well kneaded before being baked on a girdle. Chapattis are served at most Indian restaurants to eat with curry.

Char. A species of trout once quite common in English lakes and rivers and now seldom seen there. It is better known in Switzerland, the lake of Geneva being especially famed for its char (*ombre chevalier*). The fish is small, averaging about a pound, olive green on the back and with red and white spots on the lighter coloured sides. Potted char (treated as potted or soused herrings) was once a favourite dish in England.

Charcoal. A smokeless fuel giving a steady even heat and made by a special process of burning wood. Charcoal is used extensively in the Mediterranean countries, for both heating and cooking, and sometimes in England, notably for grills and out-of-door barbecues. The fumes from burning charcoal are highly poisonous and therefore dangerous, so care must be taken to have a proper outlet for them if charcoal is used indoors. Charcoal is considered an internal disinfectant; at one time charcoal biscuits were in great demand as a relief for flatulence and indigestion, due to their ability to absorb gas.

Charcuterie (French for pork butchery). A shop where various cold meats, in particular pork, are sold; e.g. brawns, galantines, tongues, sausages, etc. It is also applied as a general term to these meats.

Chard (Sea-kale Beet) (French, *blette*). A plant with long fleshy stalks topped with a spinach-like leaf. The leaves may be treated like spinach; the stalks tied in bundles and cooked like asparagus or sea-kale.

Charlotte. A pudding or cold sweet set in a plain mould resembling a deep cake tin, with slightly sloping sides widening at the top.

APPLE CHARLOTTE

The bottom and sides of the mould are lined with fingers of bread and butter arranged overlapping and the centre of the mould filled with a well-reduced purée (see MARMELADE) of apple or other stone fruit. The charlotte is then baked until the bread is golden-brown and crisp before being turned out and served hot with a fruit or custard sauce.

CHARLOTTE RUSSE

The bottom of the mould is lined with a lemon or raspberry jelly; sponge fingers or savoy biscuits are used instead of bread to line the sides; and the centre is filled with a rich BAVAROIS mixture. In Edwardian days a piece of coloured ribbon was sometimes tied round the charlotte after it was turned out.

Chartreuse. A well-known liqueur, but also a name given to a moulded dish made of one ingredient but containing a smaller quantity of choicer ingredients: e.g. chartreuse of fruit – a clear lemon jelly with grapes, strawberries, and so on set in it; or chartreuse of veal – a veal mousse with the centre filled with a salpicon of ham, tongue, and mushroom. A chartreuse may be moulded in a charlotte or ring mould.

Chasseur. Literally 'huntsman'. A name for a dish of meat or game cooked with white wine and mushrooms, strongly flavoured with tomato. Also a sauce.

Chateaubriant. A name given to a thick cut from the *cœur* or heart of a whole fillet of beef. This piece is twice as thick as an ordinary fillet steak and is ample for two people. A chateaubriant is grilled and sliced downwards for serving. *Maître-d'hôtel* butter and chateau potatoes (abbreviated from chateaubriant) are served with this steak.

Chaudfroid (literally 'hot–cold'). The name of a sauce made with milk or stock (white *chaudfroid* or brown *chaudfroid*), and a small proportion of flour and a certain amount of aspic jelly (or gelatine and stock) to make the sauce set when cold. The sauce is always used cold, coated over fish, poultry, or meat. For example, a chicken *chaudfroid* is a dish where the chicken is cooked, then jointed or left whole for stuffing (see CAPON). The joints or whole bird are coated with the sauce at setting point, two coats being used if necessary. After being decorated with sliced truffle or cooked mushroom, the whole is coated or glazed with cool liquid aspic. Brown *chaudfroid* is seldom used today but is made on the base of a *demi-glace* sauce; white *chaudfroid* is made on the base of a *béchamel*.

Chausson. French for a turnover, i.e. a round of pastry covered with apple MARMELADE, jam or fruit, and folded over. The edges are well sealed before baking. A *chausson* can also be two rounds of pastry with the filling sandwiched between. The pastry may be short or flaky. *Chaussons* are served cold.

Cheddar. A large, hard cheese much imitated. True Cheddar takes a year to mature and is made in Somerset. It keeps and travels well.

Cheese. Made from milk solids in the form of curd, it may be divided into two types, soft and hard. Soft cheeses are mostly Continental, for example, Brie, Camembert, Valmeuse, etc. Hard cheeses vary from the English Cheddar, Cheshire, and Stilton, to name only a few, to the many hard cheeses from Italy, Holland, France, and Germany. Cheeses such as Roquefort, Gorgonzola, etc. are generally classed as 'hard' though the consistency while firm should yet be creamy. See BRIE, CAMEMBERT, CHEDDAR, CHESHIRE, GORGONZOLA, GRUYÈRE, PARMESAN, ROQUEFORT, STILTON, and WENSLEYDALE.

Cherry. A decorative summer fruit coming into season in England in late June, though the imported fruit appears somewhat earlier. Most English cherries are grown in Kent and the Home

Counties; the first to appear are the May Dukes, a red, firm-fleshed cherry of which there are several varieties. Then come the white-hearts (*Bigarreau*), the best-known being Napoleons; and finally, towards the end of July or even later, the Morellos. The first two kinds are dessert cherries, the May Dukes being also suitable for compotes. White-hearts lose their colour when cooked and, moreover, have much more flavour when eaten raw.

Morellos are the finest cherries for preserving, canning, or bottling. Slightly translucent, they are full of juice, slightly acid, and tart in flavour. They are not a dessert cherry in spite of their attractive appearance. As the flesh is very juicy and tender Morellos are cut from the tree rather than pulled so that only a short piece of stalk is left attached to the cherry. If the fruit is really ripe the stone will come out with the stalk if the latter is gently pulled.

Cherry Brandy. A liqueur made from an infusion of Morello cherries in brandy.

Chervil (*Anthriscus cerefolium*). A herb with a flavour of aniseed. It is a hardy annual with sprays of small, bright green leaves and a small white flower. Because of the attractive appearance of the leaves (rather like a small maidenhair) they are frequently used as a decoration for *chaudfroids*, etc., as well as a flavouring for such sauces as *béarnaise*.

Cheshire. A hard English cow's milk cheese. It can be either red or white.

Chestnut (Spanish Chestnut). A large brown nut which when cooked has a sweet and floury kernel. Though the chestnut tree is a familiar sight in England, the nuts inside the prickly husks are too small to be worth the trouble of peeling them. Those we see in English shops are imported from France and Italy.

The kernel when cooked and sieved is dry and floury and so can be used for cakes, stuffings, and purées, both sweet and savoury. Whole, the kernels are excellent braised, and also make the famous *marrons glacés*.

Chick-Pea. One of the dried vegetables and considered (like haricot beans) to be very nutritious. In appearance they are large and yellow and need long soaking before long, slow cooking. Chick-peas are much used in Mediterranean countries in soups and stews.

Chicken. This bird is classed as poultry (see also FOWL) and has certain stages of growth at which it is killed and sold. Chickens are bred specially for the table and also as laying birds. Fresh poultry is sold at dressed weight, that is plucked and drawn but including the giblets. The weight of oven-ready birds is marked on them when they are sold.

Poussin. A bird 4–6 weeks old and 1–1¼ lb. in weight. May be prepared in many ways; roast, boned and stuffed, pot-roast, split and grilled, etc. One is allowed per person. A double poussin, 8–10 weeks old and 1¾–2 lb. in weight, will serve two.

Spring Chicken or Broiler. A bird 3 months old and 2–2½ lb. in weight. Prepared as poussins, and for sautés.

Roasting Chicken. A bird up to one year old, 3–4 lb. in weight. May be used for most chicken dishes.

Boiling Fowl. A bird 15–18 months old, and generally one which has been laying.

Cockerel. This should be killed at 6 months, unless caponized. (See CAPON.)

Chicken Turbot. See TURBOT.

Chicory (*Cichorium endiva*). Known as *endive* in France. (What in England is called endive, the curly endive used mostly as a green salad during the late winter and early spring, in France is *chicorée frisée*.) Chicory is one of the vegetables of which the stems are blanched when growing, and it is delicious raw or cooked. Largely imported from Belgium, it is in season from November to March.

A different variety of chicory, *Intybus*, is grown to adulterate coffee. The root only is used, first roasted, then ground and mixed with the coffee.

Chiffonnade (French *chiffon*, 'a rag'). A term used to describe a shredded green vegetable, lettuce, spinach, sorrel, etc. Egg mayonnaise can be arranged on a *chiffonnade*, i.e. shredded lettuce.

Chilli. See CAPSICUM. *Chilli powder* is ground from the small red chilli.

Chine. From the French *échine*, meaning the back-bone of the animal, containing the spinal cord. The chine bone is the end bone on the ribs or loin and is usually sawn through by the butcher for easy removal before the joint is sliced into cutlets or roasted whole.

Chinese Gooseberry. Brown-skinned oval fruit, like a small sausage, and with flesh and seeds not unlike a gooseberry. The flavour is somewhat the same. Chinese gooseberries appear in shops late November to January.

Chip. Fried potatoes: *Allumettes* – match-shaped pieces. Chips or *Pont neuf* – cut into thick 'fingers'. Game chips – wafer-thin slices of potatoes. Straw or *Pommes pailles* – cut into very thin strips.

Chipolata. A corruption of the French word *ciboule* (a kind of chive), and in Italian cooking denoting a rich ragout well flavoured with onion. Now chipolata has come to mean an especially small sausage.

Chitterling. Small scraps or trimmings of offal from a freshly killed pig, which are fried. Chitterlings can also be the intestines of any animal.

Chive (*Allium schoenoprasum*). Classed as a pot-herb. Small clumps of tiny bulbs clustered together, with fleshy green shoots and purple flowers. The shoots are the only part of the plant used and should be cut with scissors. Chives have a delicate flavour of onion and are particularly useful in salads and stuffings. The plants themselves make a good border to the herb garden and grow well, too, in a pot or window-box.

Chocolate. Made from cocoa. Chocolate-making is a highly skilled process, and chocolate varies in quality and price according to the milling and the amount of starch and sugar added. It is sold in block or powdered form. The former is the most useful in the kitchen and should be of good quality, that is, not too sweet. There is some confusion about the terms plain and unsweetened chocolate: plain chocolate, obtainable through the retail trade, contains a proportion of sugar; while unsweetened or bitter chocolate, sold only through wholesalers, has, as the name implies, no sugar.

Chop. A piece, about 1–1½ inches thick, chopped from the loin of lamb, mutton, pork, or veal. A chump chop (two in each loin) is taken from the end of the loin nearest the tail and contains more bone (the pelvic bone) than an ordinary chop.

Chou. The name given to a paste of butter, flour, and eggs (French, *pâte à chou*). It may be baked in teaspoonfuls (*petits choux*) and filled with cream or *crème pâtissière*, or fried in teaspoonfuls (*beignets*) and served as a sweet or savoury with an appropriate sauce. Chou paste is one of the most important basic mixtures in cookery.

Choucroute. The French term for SAUERKRAUT – fermented cabbage. *Choucroute garnie* is a dish of the cabbage garnished with Frankfurter sausages, boiled knuckle of pork, salted belly of pork, etc.

Chowder. A speciality of the eastern seaboard of the United States. The main ingredients are different kinds of shellfish – clams, lobster, etc. – or white fish, onions, potatoes, and salt pork. Like *bouillabaisse* it is a soup stew and should be made with freshly caught fish. There are many variations.

Chump. See CHOP.

Chutney. A condiment of Indian origin made with a mixture of sweet and sour ingredients – fruit, vinegar, sugar, and spices – stewed slowly together, then potted for long keeping. Fresh chutneys, which do not keep, can be made quickly for serving immediately, always with the sweet and sour flavour in mind. Both sorts can be mild or hot according to taste.

Cider. Apple wine or fermented juice of apples, made in countries where apples are cultivated extensively, i.e. Normandy, parts of the United States of America and Canada, and England. Apples are crushed or milled, and the pulp is pressed well in a cider mill to extract the juice. This is then run into barrels to ferment. When fermentation has ceased the cider is bottled. Good draught cider in the place of its origin is considered superior to the bottled variety, and is strong and heady. It is also the best for cooking: a glass added to a soup or stew, or used to make the batter for apple fritters, greatly improves the dish. As a drink it is popular either straight or in a cup or punch. See also VINEGAR.

Cinnamon (*Cinnamomum zeylanicum*). The bark of the cinnamon tree. It may be bought powdered or in short sticks. A piece of cinnamon stick is used to flavour mulled wine, spiced fruits, sweet pickles, and so on. Powdered or ground cinnamon is used in very small quantities to flavour apples and other fruit, and cakes, biscuits, or pastry.

Citron. A large lemon-like fruit. Its thick rind is especially suitable for candying, when it appears dark green in colour with a translucent pulp. A few thin slices of the peel are the traditional finish to a Madeira cake. It is one of the components of the 'mixed peel' used for fruit or plum cakes.

Civet. French for a rich ragout of game. The best-known is *civet de lièvre*, the equivalent of jugged hare.

Clafouti. A cherry and batter sweet from Provence. Black or red cherries are stoned and laid in a baking-dish, and a thick batter is poured over them. The whole is then baked.

Clam. A shellfish well known and esteemed in America, and though it can be found on English shores it is less common there than in the U.S. Clams may be cooked and eaten as mussels, but are, above all, the most famous ingredient of the CHOWDER.

Claret. The name given in England to red BORDEAUX wines, a cheap and popular drink there during the seventeenth and eighteenth centuries.

Clarify. To make clear or to free from impurities. Frying fat or dripping may be cleaned by being melted and having about a third of their amount of water added. This mixture is then boiled for a time before being strained. When cold the cake of clean fat is carefully removed, leaving the water and other impurities behind. (See also BUTTER.) Sweet and savoury jellies, and meat broths (e.g. consommé) are clarified by the addition of egg-whites to the cold liquid. These are well whisked into the liquid while it is being brought to the boil, at which point the coagulated albumen will rise to the top as scum, collecting any opaque particles. After standing, the whole is poured through a cloth or jelly bag. If not entirely clear the liquid is taken up and poured again over the collected scum or filter in the bag or cloth.

Clementine. See ORANGE.

Clod. See BEEF.

Clove (*Eugenia carophyllata*). An aromatic spice much used for seasoning, either ground or whole. The clove is the dried flower bud of a small shrub-like tree mostly cultivated in the Moluccas or Spice Islands. A clove is so called because it resembles a nail, from the Latin *clovus* – French *clou*.

Clove is also the name given to a segment of a root of garlic. This term has no connexion with the spice, but is derived from the verb to cleave, or to split up.

Coal-Fish (or Coly or Saithe). A fish resembling a haddock or cod, with a black skin, and rather greyish flesh which whitens during cooking. Caught mostly in northern waters, it is at its best when eaten young and small in size.

Cob-Nut. See FILBERT.

Cochineal. See CARMINE.

Cockerel. See CHICKEN.

Cockle. A small mollusc with a white, ribbed, hinged shell. Cockles are usually sold ready cooked from stalls where other shellfish such as whelks and mussels are also found. They are sprinkled with vinegar and eaten with fresh bread and butter.

Cocoa. The ripe fruit of the cocoa tree which is cultivated in tropical countries. It is pod-like in shape and contains the seeds, or nibs, from which the cocoa is made. These are roasted and then milled. The nib contains a fairly high proportion of a yellowish, sweet-smelling fat which when extracted hardens into a cake and is known as *cocoa butter*. It is the extraction or addition of this together with starch and sugar to the ground cocoa which varies the quality of cocoa and chocolate. *Cocoa powder*, sweetened or unsweetened, is most commonly used as a drink. It is less rich and so more digestible than chocolate. An infusion which is especially suitable for children can also be made from the cocoa nib.

Coconut. The fruit of a palm tree (*Cocas nucifera*) growing in tropical climates, particularly the eastern parts of Asia and the East Indies. The nut is large with a hairy husk and tough shell. Inside, the flesh is snowy white and crisp. When grated it is added to curries and chutneys. For confectionery and cakes, dried or desiccated coconut is best. The nut also contains a small quantity of liquid, coconut milk, greenish-white in colour, refreshing to drink but of little value otherwise. This should not be confused with the 'coconut milk' mentioned in curry recipes: this is an infusion of grated coconut and has more flavour than the natural milk.

Cod. A deep-sea fish in season all the year round, but at its best from May to October. It has fine, creamy flakes and lends itself to many ways of cooking. The fresh fish can be bought whole, in fillets, or in steaks as it can weigh from $1\frac{1}{4}$ to 20 lb.; the best weigh 9–10 lb. The roe is sold separately, either fresh or smoked.

The liver is used in the manufacture of cod-liver oil, and the tongues are considered a great delicacy. Fillets of cod are also sold smoked. These are good, although not to be compared with smoked haddock, and can be cooked in the same way. Cod is also salted: the fish is split, salted, and dried, and exported in large quantities to France, Spain, and Italy, where it has a more ready sale than in England. Salt cod must be thoroughly washed and soaked before it is cooked. The true BRANDADE is prepared with this fish.

Some people think the flesh of cod dull and watery but this is invariably due to lack of skill in cooking, and if the following treatment is given before attempting even the most simple recipe, it is fit to grace any table. Wash and dry the fish, rub the skin with cut fresh lemon, and sprinkle lightly with salt. Leave in a cool place for $\frac{1}{2}$–1 hour, then tip away the liquid, wipe the fish, and follow the chosen recipe.

Coffee. The dried bean of the coffee plant or tree. The fruit or coffee berry resembles a cherry which when dried and split open contains two greenish coloured beans. In order to bring out the characteristic flavour the beans are roasted before being ground and infused in water to make coffee. The degree of roasting and of grinding varies according to the flavour required and the way the coffee is made. The most usual roasts are medium, and French or Continental roast, the latter being dark, almost burnt. Grinding should be medium for percolators and fine or filter ground for filtered coffee. There are other grinds as well as different roasts but these depend on personal taste. There are more opinions and arguments as to the brewing of coffee than almost any other culinary process, and most people have their favourite blend of coffee and special way of making it. See also CHICORY.

Cognac. A small town in the Charente district of France. The name Cognac is given to an *eau-de-vie* distilled from the wines of the region. Cognac implies a fine brandy as opposed to the lesser qualities. See BRANDY and EAU-DE-VIE.

Cointreau. A French liqueur made with oranges.

Colcannon. Chopped cooked cabbage and mashed potato beaten together with butter and hot milk until light and fluffy. Originally an Irish dish.

Cole Slaw. Originally an American dish. Crisp shredded cabbage is chilled and served with cream or mayonnaise. It may be garnished with slices of apple or green peppers.

Coly. See COAL-FISH.

Compote. A dish of fruit poached in syrup, e.g. apricot, apple, gooseberry, etc.

Concasser. Literally to chop roughly. The term is usually applied to tomatoes, and they should first be skinned, and squeezed to remove the seeds.

Condensed Milk. Tinned milk. This may be sweetened or unsweetened though milk sold as condensed is sweetened, and evaporated unsweetened.

Condiment. Any spice or bottled sauce which adds piquancy or flavour to a dish, e.g. salt, pepper, mustard.

Conger Eel. See EEL.

Consommé. A clear strong soup made of a beef and bone stock which has been enriched, concentrated, and clarified. Consommé may be garnished in a number of ways: perhaps the best known are *petite marmite* (with chicken) and *consommé à la royale* (see ROYALE).

Continental Sausages. Numerous varieties are now on sale in England, the better-known of which are listed below. Nearly all of them are made of pork.

Garlic. French. A sausage about 2½–3 in. in diameter, made of salted pork or ham, and strongly flavoured with garlic.
Liver. These sausages are made in France, Belgium, and Germany and vary a little in size and price. All are rich and full of flavour.
Mortadella. A large type of sausage of Italian origin, but also made in

France. It should be sliced thinly before being served with other cold meats.

Salami. Made in Italy, Hungary, and Germany, and varies a little from place to place. Has a speckled appearance when sliced due to the pin-points of fat among the red meat. Piquant in flavour, with a varying proportion of garlic.

All these are used as an *hors-d'œuvre* or part of an *hors-d'œuvre*. FRANKFURTERS and SAVELOYS, however, are not.

Coriander. The fruit of *Coriandrum sativum*, much used in spiced dishes such as curry. The fruit is generally used dried and is crushed or powdered before being added to a dish. The whole seeds may be candied in sugar and made into comfits. Ripe coriander seeds may be used fresh, as may the leaves, but sparingly as the flavour is oily and pungent.

Corned Beef. Salt boiled beef. The word 'corned' denotes a salt meat, and is derived from the 'corns', small pieces or crystals of coarse salt used for pickling.

Cornet. See MOULD.

Cornish Pasty. A round of shortcrust or flaky pastry folded and shaped like a TURNOVER with a filling of meat, potatoes and onions and then baked. A pasty may be large enough for 3–4 people or of individual size.

Cornflour. The finely ground kernel of Indian corn or maize. Cornflour is a fine starch and mixed with wheat flour is used to make cakes. It is also used for blancmanges and for thickening sauces, gravies, etc., although for this arrowroot is better as it is a finer starch and cooks instantly when the liquid boils.

Corn on the Cob. See INDIAN CORN.

Corn Salad (Lamb's Lettuce). A small annual plant (*Valerianella olitoria*) useful as a salad vegetable in winter as it is not harmed by frost. The whole plant is pulled or cut from the ground, and should be washed well to remove all grit, as it is low-growing. Corn salad is inclined to be dull if eaten by itself, and so is best mixed with other winter salads, chicory, beetroot, or celery.

Cos Lettuce. See LETTUCE.

Coulibiaca (Russian cookery). A mixture of flaked salmon and rice wrapped round with a brioche dough or puff pastry. Shaped into a long fat roll and well glazed with beaten egg, a *coulibiaca* is baked and served hot with a cream or suprême sauce.

Coulis. A French word meaning a soup-stew, or liquid thick with pieces of vegetable or meat. In old English cookery books the word 'cullis' is found; this has fallen into disuse and *coulis* has taken its place.

Coupe. A shallow cup in glass or silver, usually on a low stem, used for serving ices or fresh fruit salad; e.g. Coupe Jacques, fruit covered with ices of various flavours, sometimes a mixture of water and cream ice.

Courgette (Zucchini). A variety of baby marrow, about 4–5 in. long. Courgettes are cooked whole without being peeled and have a fresh and delicate flavour. They are easily grown and call for the same treatment as marrows. They are in season at the same time in England, but are imported during most of the year.

Court-Bouillon. A slightly acidulated stock made with water, root vegetables, and wine or vinegar. Used primarily for poaching fish to give flavour and to keep the flesh a good colour. Used also for veal, e.g. calf's head.

Cous-cous. An Arabian dish, a sort of farinaceous stew, made from millet flour cooked with water until dry and fluffy and served with a mutton stew. The cous-cous flour can also be boiled in a cloth with the mutton and vegetables.

Crab. A popular and moderately priced shellfish with large claws and a rough shell. In season from early May to September. Crabs are sold ready cooked, and their quality judged by their weight. The large claws contain the white meat, the brown lying in the big shell. Crabs vary from 1 to 3½ lb. in weight, the cocks being considered the finest as their claws are bigger than the hens'. A disadvantage is that they must be dressed, or prepared for serving, which takes time. Full directions for this are given in most cookery books, and fishmongers will on occasion do it for a small extra charge. Crab meat may also be bought by the pound from big stores, both white and brown, though a freshly dressed crab is naturally the best for serving as a salad with mayonnaise or French dressing. Crab meat may also be served hot, devilled or in a soufflé.

Crab-apple. A wild apple of bitter flavour grown in gardens chiefly for decoration. The blossom is white or pale pink and the fruit golden-yellow to scarlet according to the variety. The fruit is ideal for making jelly or for pickling whole as a spiced fruit.

Crackling. The skin of pork when roasted. The skin must be scored before roasting, i.e. slit at intervals about $\frac{1}{4}$ in. apart with the point of a sharp knife.

Cranberry. This fruit grows wild, but those marketed are cultivated. The plant is like a bilberry and its natural habitat is on heathy moorland or hills. It is much esteemed in the making of sauces or jelly to serve with duck or turkey or as a compote.

Crapaudine (*Crapaud*, French for toad). The French equivalent to the English spatchcock, i.e. small birds split down the back and flattened.

Crawfish (French, *langouste*). A large crustacean much esteemed on the Continent. Crawfish are larger than lobsters, growing up to 5 or 6 lb., and the flesh is correspondingly coarser. Unlike lobsters they have small claws and all the meat lies in the tail. Because of their size they lend themselves particularly well to ornamental dishes for a cold table.

Crayfish (French, *écrevisse*). A small fresh-water shellfish greatly prized in the Scandinavian countries, where a festival is held every year in its honour. It is like a miniature lobster and is usually boiled and served plainly with a dressing and brown bread and butter.

Cream. The 'top of the milk', i.e. the fat which rises to the surface of the milk. Milk which is to be set for cream should not be pasteurized (i.e. heat-treated). This, though killing any possible tubercle bacilli, also destroys the lactic germ, and milk thus treated does not sour easily, nor does the cream separate so easily from the milk. To obtain cream, milk used to be poured into large shallow pans and left for 12 hours or so for the cream to rise. It was then taken off with a special skimmer. Nowadays the milk is put through a separator which can be adjusted to extract all the fats from the milk or only a certain proportion, thus giving thick (double) or thin (single) cream. Commercial creameries now adjust the fat content of cream to give different grades.

Cream is used to a large extent in cooking, either plain added to sauces, or whipped for cold soufflés, creams, etc. It is also the main ingredient of BUTTER.

SOUR CREAM
Used for butter-making and cream cheese and in certain mid-European dishes, e.g. GOULASH, BORSHCH, etc.

CLOTTED CREAM
Devonshire or Cornish clotted cream. This is obtained by heating fresh milk very gradually in shallow bowls to scalding point. The milk should first be allowed to stand for at least 12 hours for the cream to rise. After heating the milk is left for some hours before the cream is skimmed off. Devonshire cream varies slightly from the Cornish in that it is smoother and more solid. Cornish is rough-textured, with a more pronounced taste of scalded cream.

Cream of Tartar. Bitartrate of potassium. Mixed with bicarbonate of soda it becomes a raising agent, because when it is moistened carbonic-acid gas is generated. (See BAKING-POWDER.) A pinch of cream of tartar may also be added to boiling syrup instead of liquid glucose, to prevent graining.

Crécy. A town in France famous for the carrots grown in the surrounding country. Certain dishes which contain carrots in some form are called *à la Crécy*.

Crème Chantilly. See CHANTILLY.

Crème de Menthe. A peppermint-flavoured LIQUEUR.

Crème Pâtissière. See PASTRY CREAM.

Crémet. A milk curd made in the Dauphinois district of France. The characteristic is that the milk 'turns' and 'jells' quickly without getting too sour. Once firm the curd is beaten up with fresh cream and egg-whites and sweetened. It is then put into small perforated pots, covered with muslin and left to drain in a cool place.

Creole. Chicken or meat with a garnish of rice cooked as a pilaff with peppers and tomatoes.

Crêpe. See PANCAKE.

Crêpe Suzette. A wafer-thin pancake prepared from a batter flavoured with an orange liqueur, such as curaçao. When cooked the pancakes are spread with butter worked with sugar and the zest and juice of a tangerine or orange. It may also be flavoured with the same liqueur. The pancakes are then folded, heated and flamed with brandy or orange liqueur.

Cress. Garden cress (*Lepidium satirum*), an annual, is commonly sold in small punnets, and may easily be grown in small seed boxes or on damp flannel kept indoors. It grows quickly and is useful for salads, sandwiches and garnishing. See also MUSTARD and WATERCRESS.

Croissant. A rich, flaky, crescent-shaped roll. The dough of flour, milk and water is first raised with yeast, then a generous proportion of butter is added and the paste rolled and finished as for puff pastry.

Croque-en-Bouche (literally, 'crack-in-the-mouth'). An ornamental sweet made only as a decorative piece for a buffet or reception. Small cooked crisp balls of chou pastry or meringues are stuck together with a sugar syrup boiled to the crack stage (see SYRUP). These are built up to form a pyramid 7–8 in. high. The interior may be left empty or filled with crème Chantilly. The top may be finished off with a plume of spun sugar.

Croquette. A savoury mixture of chopped cooked chicken, hard-boiled eggs, or flaked fish bound with a thick *béchamel* sauce. It is shaped into balls, flat rounds, or cork shapes, coated with egg and breadcrumbs, and fried in deep fat. See RISSOLE.

Croustade. A case of fried bread to contain any savoury mixture. A *croustade* of sweetbreads or of buttered eggs and prawns may be served as a savoury. The case is made either from a whole loaf with the crust removed or from rounds 2½–3 in. wide stamped out from slices of bread 1½–2 in. thick. A small cutter or knife-point then makes an incision in the middle of the loaf or round. After the bread has been fried in deep fat, the centre is scooped out to form a case. The *croustade* is not necessarily eaten.

Croûte. A small round of bread, fried or toasted, on which a savoury mixture is arranged. It is also used to garnish a dish, e.g. a sauté where the crisp bread makes a good contrast to the rich gravy. See also CANAPÉ.

Croûton. A small square or dice of fried bread, or sometimes fried potato, to accompany cream or purée soups.

Crowdie. Scots name for a cheese made from the soured curd of milk.

Crudités. Raw vegetables such as radishes, spring onions, baby carrots, etc. set on the table before a lunch.

Crumpet. A thick flat 'pancake' 3 inches in diameter, smooth on the under side and full of small holes on the upper side. They are made from a batter of flour, water, and yeast which is poured into special rings set on a heated baking-sheet, and baked in a fairly quick oven. When done they are pale, a creamy white in colour, and soft, and need re-cooking. Crumpets may be bought at most bakers' during the winter months; they must be toasted, well buttered, and served piping hot. They may also be fried with bacon.

Crustacea. A collective word for all shellfish.

Crystallization. A process connected with confectionery. Crystallization on fondant creams, flowers, and glacé fruits forms a protective coating as well as giving an attractive appearance, and though the process is simple, great care is required to get a good result. Moreover, special equipment is necessary: a thermometer, saccharometer, and crystallizing tray or tins. The process is as follows: a thick syrup is made according to what is to be crystallized, usually 220°–224° F., and 32°–36° on the saccharometer, and this is then cooled to room temperature. The fondants are placed carefully in the crystallizing trays. The lukewarm syrup is poured over them, and the sweets are left to soak for the prescribed time, when a uniform coating of crystals should have formed. After the syrup is drained off the fondants are left to dry on racks. Crystallization continues throughout the draining and drying process.

Cucumber. A vegetable of the melon family, eaten either as a salad or cooked. Grown under glass, cucumbers are at their best from May to September, though available throughout the year. Small ridge cucumbers grown out of doors in late summer are used chiefly for pickling, i.e. dill cucumbers.

Cuisson. The cooking juices from fish, chicken, or meat.

Cullis. See COULIS.

Cummin (*Cumminum cyminum*). Aromatic seeds very like caraway in appearance and flavour. Used for flavouring and in the preparation of liqueurs.

Curaçao. A LIQUEUR made from the rind of Seville oranges and gin or brandy.

Curds. Milk solids which form when milk turns acid, i.e. sour, or when acid is added and the milk is warmed (e.g. curds for cheese-making). Curds can also form when the milk is sweet and rennet is added (JUNKET). Firmer curds made by souring are the base of milk cheeses (e.g. CROWDIE) and hard curds artificially induced by cheese rennet are used for all cheese-making.

Curing. A process to preserve meat by dry salting or by pickling (see BRINE). Salt is the most important ingredient in curing though other substances such as saltpetre and sugar are added. The proportion of saltpetre to salt is small and gives the pink colour to meat. Too much saltpetre hardens the meat and the sugar is added to counteract this and to give flavour. In the case of bacon, hams, etc., this process of preservation is continued by smoking. Fish such as haddock, bloaters and kippers are also salted or cured before smoking.

Currant. A summer fruit, acid in flavour. The most esteemed variety is the *black-currant* which contains large quantities of vitamin C. Black-currants are preserved in various forms – bottled, in jams, and in syrups – and are also used for making CASSIS. *Red-currants* are most frequently used in red-currant jelly to serve with meat and game, and in syrups for long drinks. The juice is valued for its high pectin content. *White-currants* are seldom marketed, but are most commonly used in jellies, syrups, and various sweets. Dried currants are the fruit of the Corinth grape.

Curry. A hot dish or sauce hailing from India and the Far East. Curry powder is a generic term for a combination of several different spices thoroughly dried and ground and made up according to the locality and the type of food to be 'curried'. In England curry powder may be bought already compounded but in the countries of its origin the spices are pounded and mixed as they are needed.

Custard. Custard is made of eggs, either yolks only or a mixture of whole eggs and yolks, and milk. It may be a sweet sauce to serve with fruit or a hot pudding, or the base of a cold soufflé or cream; in both cases yolks and milk only are used. As a pudding in its own right (custard pudding or caramel custard), whole eggs are mixed with yolks and milk, the egg-whites setting the pudding and the yolks giving the creamy texture.

Cutlet. A delicious piece of meat taken from the rib-bone of the best end or top rib of lamb or mutton; a veal cutlet is taken from the same part of the animal, but can also come from a thick piece of the veal fillet, i.e. from the leg. Cutlets may be grilled or pan-fried and lend themselves to many different entrées.

Cutlet Bat. A heavy flat piece of metal with a handle, used for flattening cutlets, veal escalopes, sole fillets, etc. before cooking.

Cuttlefish. See OCTOPUS.

Dab. A small flat fish found on sandy shores round the English coasts. Dabs are a species of FLOUNDER but are usually smaller, around 4–6 oz. in weight, or less.

Damson. A small purple plum. Damsons ripen later than most plums, from late August to mid-September. They are not good eaten raw, but have a delicious rich flavour when cooked. They make excellent compotes, jams, jellies or fruit cheeses, in fact preserves of every kind.

Dandelion. Well known as a weed, but the young leaves, if blanched like chicory, make an excellent salad. Dandelions may be specially cultivated in order to get large strong plants; more simply, flower-pots can be inverted over young plants growing as weeds in order to exclude the light. When thoroughly white the crisp leaves are used, either by themselves or with other salad greens, dressed with oil and vinegar.

Dariole. See MOULD.

Darne. A French term for the thick cut of fish taken from the middle of salmon, cod, turbot, weighing 2 lb. or more.

D'Artois. The name given to two pieces of puff pastry filled with pastry cream and fruit (e.g. apricots), baked, and cut into slices.

Date. A dried fruit from the date palm cultivated chiefly in North Africa. Soft, sweet, and pulpy, dates are a popular dessert fruit for Christmas; specially selected fruit are packed in oblong boxes, while dates of a lesser quality are stoned and compressed, and then sold by the pound for cakes and puddings. Dates are considered highly nutritious.

Daube. A French term used to describe meat, generally beef, that is braised gently in red wine for some hours and well seasoned with herbs.

Dauphinois. Generally denotes a dish containing milk or cream and cheese, e.g. *gratin dauphinois*, a dish of thinly sliced potatoes, milk, and Gruyère cheese baked in the oven.

Deglaze (French, *déglacer*). To rinse out, usually with stock or wine, a roasting-tin or pan to remove the deposits or sediment of glaze left by roasting or sautéing meat or game.

Dégorger. This process is used to prepare aubergines, cucumber, etc. The vegetables are lightly salted after slicing, left for an hour or so, and then drained well. Further cooking or preparation can then be carried out. Like blanching, this process removes any strong taste.

Demi-Deuil (literally 'half-mourning'). A chicken or turkey cooked *en demi-deuil* has thin slices of truffle pushed up under the skin on to the breast. The bird is left for some hours before roasting so that the perfume of the truffle permeates the flesh.

Demi-Glace (literally 'half-glaze'). A name given, particularly in big kitchens, to a rich brown sauce made with bone stock. The sauce is reduced to a syrupy consistency and so forms a half-glaze when coated over meat or game entrées. It is also served as an accompanying sauce to roasts or grills. See BROWN SAUCE.

Dépouiller (literally 'to skin'). The term for a process used in the making of a brown or *demi-glace* sauce. Dashes of cold stock are added at intervals to the sauce as it simmers and cause any scum or grease to rise to the surface. This is at once skimmed off and the process repeated until the sauce becomes semi-clear and a rich brown.

Dessert. The last course of a meal (see MENU). At a formal dinner the table is cleared for dessert: the cloth is removed and all cutlery and salt, pepper, and mustard pots are taken off. A dessert plate and finger bowl together with a silver dessert knife and fork are placed in front of each guest, and the fruit in season handed round. Nuts and dried fruits may also be put on the table together with a dessert wine, e.g. port. Nowadays dessert can mean the sweet course.

Devil. Signifies spiced, peppery, and hot in taste. Devilled bones are drumsticks or thigh meat of chicken, turkey, or game, highly seasoned by being marinaded in a mixture of bottled sauces such as Worcester sauce or mushroom ketchup. Fish and shellfish can be treated in the same way. For a 'dry devil' the meat is liberally peppered and spread with mustard. The joints in both cases are then either fried in a little butter or dripping, or well brushed with melted butter and grilled. The meat or joints should be very well browned, almost charred, before serving.

Dhal. A purée of lentils well seasoned and flavoured with a little green ginger or curry powder. One of the accompaniments to a curry.

Dill (*Anethum graveolens*). An annual feathery grey-green herb, resembling fennel in appearance and flavour, though more delicate. The leaves are used for garnishing or are chopped and added to mayonnaise and other sauces, served mostly with fish. The stalks are used for flavouring pickles, e.g. dill cucumber.

Dolmas (Turkish cookery). A small portion of minced meat and sometimes rice wrapped in vine leaves or blanched cabbage leaves and cooked in stock. Both versions may be finished in a strong tomato sauce.

Dough. A mixture of flour and liquid (water or milk) used for making bread or scones. A dough should be very light and pliable. See KNEADING.

Doughnut. A bun or bread dough rolled into balls the size of a small egg. A spoonful of firm jam should be pressed into the middle of each before it is fried in deep fat and rolled in caster sugar. Doughnuts may also be ring-shaped.

61

Dragée. A sugar-coated sweetmeat; e.g. almond dragées, whole almonds coated with hard sugar, which may be white or coloured pink or mauve.

Drambuie. A Scottish LIQUEUR made from whisky and honey.

Dredge. To sprinkle flour, sugar, etc. from a container with a perforated top. The size of the holes depends on what is to be dredged. For example, a flour dredger has large holes; caster-sugar dredger, fine holes; and an icing-sugar dredger, very fine holes.

Dripping. The fat from roasting meat. Beef dripping is generally considered the best and may be used not only for roasting meat but for frying and as a shortening for pastry and fruit cakes. Dripping must be kept clean and free from any liquid. When poured from the roasting or dripping tin it should be strained into a bowl and left to set. The cake of fat can then be taken out and the gravy carefully scraped away from the bottom. This can be used for enriching gravies, brown soups, and stews. *Dripping toast*, rounds of toasted bread well spread with beef dripping together with the gravy and then heated in the oven until piping hot, is a nursery tea-time favourite.

Drop Scone (or Pancake). A flat spongy scone about $\frac{1}{4}$–$\frac{1}{2}$ in. thick and $2\frac{1}{2}$ inches in diameter and made from a thick batter of flour, eggs, and milk. They are cooked on a girdle. Drop scones can also be the size of a teaplate and barely $\frac{1}{4}$ in. thick. They are known as pancakes in Scotland.

Duchesse. Now usually refers to potatoes cooked in the following manner and used either for garnishing or as an accompaniment. A good potato purée is made and an egg-yolk added with butter and hot milk. The purée is then piped on to buttered baking-sheets in rosettes, and these are brushed lightly with beaten egg and browned in the oven. Duchesse potatoes may also be piped directly on to a serving dish to form a border. This is then browned, after which the centre is filled with a salpicon of sweetbreads, suprême of chicken, and so on.

Duck. A water bird of which there are two varieties – the domestic type, bred specially for the table, and the wild duck. Of the domestic duck (classed as poultry) the large white Aylesbury duck is the most prized. The dressed weight averages between 4 and 5 lb., but as there is less meat on a duck than on a chicken a duck of this size is enough for only four people. Thanks to the deep freeze, ducks are now available all the year round. Though there are several ways of cooking them, perhaps the best is to roast them, either with the traditional stuffing of sage and onion, and apple sauce, or unstuffed with an orange sauce (see BIGARADE) or orange salad to accompany.

WILD DUCKS make brief appearances in the shops but are not so popular as domestic ducks, as they have a pronounced fishy flavour. They, too, are best roasted, but left *saignant* and served with a sharp sauce and an orange salad.

Dugléré. A way of cooking and serving white fish, such as turbot, sole, etc. The fish is poached in white wine and water and a sauce made of the liquid. Cream is added and the sauce finished with chopped parsley and concasséd tomatoes.

Dulse. A red-brown edible seaweed. It is stewed like LAVER.

Dumpling. A paste of flour, salt, and water which is formed into small balls and simmered in boiling water or stock. Suet dumplings are a classic accompaniment to boiled beef. Dumplings are popular in Germany and are made with different ingredients, bread, shortcrust, and so on, both sweet and savoury.

Duxelles. A mince of mushrooms with a little chopped shallot, and herbs. A duxelles can be made of whole mushrooms, or stalks and peelings, finely chopped. These are cooked in a nut of butter with the shallot and herbs until any liquid has evaporated, but leaving the mixture nicely moist. After seasoning the duxelles may be used to flavour stuffings, sauces, and soups.

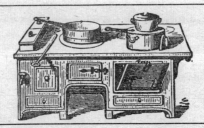

E

Eau-de-Vie. Alcohol produced from the distillation of wine, the most famous of which is COGNAC, distilled from the wines of Charente. (See also BRANDY.) *Eau-de-vie* also forms the base of many liqueurs.

Eccles Cake. A rich fruit mixture (currants and candied peel) put between two rounds of flaky pastry approximately 4 inches in diameter. Once the edges are sealed the cake is turned over and flattened with the rolling-pin but kept in a round. Three slashes are made on the top of each and the surface glazed with egg-white and sugar before baking. BANBURY CAKES are made in the same way but shaped differently. The filling is put on one round only, then the edges are gathered up and pinched together. The cake is turned over and rolled to an oblong before glazing and baking.

Éclair. A fat finger length of chou paste baked until crisp and then filled with either chocolate, coffee, or vanilla-flavoured pastry cream. The top is finished with a fondant of glacé icing to match the filling. Éclairs may also be filled with whipped cream, but traditionally pastry cream is used.

Écrevisse. French for CRAYFISH.

Eel. A fish commonly found in both fresh and salt water. Perhaps the best known is the fresh-water eel, averaging 1½–2 lb. in weight and imported in large quantities from Holland, where it is even more popular than in England. Smoked eels, also imported, are a delicacy, served thinly sliced as a first course. The huge conger eel, sometimes up to 20 feet in length, lives in salt water. The flesh is firm and well-flavoured. It is an ingredient of *bouillabaisse*, and at one time was a favourite in fried fish shops.

Egg. Of all basic ingredients in the kitchen eggs are among the most valuable. They have a high protein content, and so make a balanced meal at a low price. Essential in cakes and puddings they can also be cooked in so many forms that they seldom become boring. They should be eaten as fresh as possible; those not 'new-laid', i.e. more than a week old, are best used in cooking. A simple test to find out if an egg is really new-laid is that when it is broken the white clings to the yolk. The staler the egg the more liquid the white.

Hens' eggs are the most widely used, but during the spring and summer both duck and goose eggs are available. Duck eggs are nowadays slightly suspect as they can have unpleasant effects unless they are really fresh. Duck eggs are of real value in the kitchen. They are larger than hens' eggs, averaging a good 2½ oz. each, and are excellent for cake-making, especially if used whole. The whites do not whip quite so readily as those of hens' eggs. Goose eggs are admirable for scrambling or making omelets, one egg being sufficient for two people.

Eggplant. See AUBERGINE.

Elderberry. The fruit of the elder (*Sambucus*). The small black berries ripen in September and are used for making wine, jelly, or syrup.

Elderflower. The flowers of the elder have an unpleasant heady scent, but infused in syrup or in a jelly give a delicious flavour of muscat grapes. This goes particularly well with gooseberries, and a few flowers tied in muslin and put with the fruit while stewing will give the right amount of flavour. Elderflower syrup is made by infusing the flowers in a syrup with a few gooseberries to give sharpness; then it is strained, bottled, and sterilized for keeping. Two or three spoonfuls of this will give a delicious flavour to a fruit salad or to fresh strawberries. Wine can also be made from elderflowers.

C

Emmenthal. See GRUYÈRE.

Endive. See CHICORY.

Entrecôte. A French term for the top part of the sirloin or ribs of beef. The cut is tender and full of flavour, and may be cooked as a small roast or cut into steaks.

Entrée. A term now somewhat out of date, but signifying a dish preceding the roast in a menu and following the fish course. An entrée is also a made-up dish which is complete in itself, e.g. a meat dish with a vegetable garnish or a *vol-au-vent* of sweetbreads, and usually calls for some skill in cooking. Nowadays an entrée appears as the main course in a menu.

Entremets (literally 'between dishes'). An entremets can be either a dressed vegetable, e.g. asparagus, globe artichoke, etc. served as a separate course after the main dish, or a sweet.

Epigramme. Epigrammes are small pieces taken from the best end of neck or breast of lamb, simmered until tender, then boned and pressed. When cold they are dipped in egg and breadcrumbs and grilled or fried. A piquant sauce should accompany them.

Escalope. A term generally applied to a thin piece of meat (usually veal) cut from the leg or fillet, and cooked in various ways.

Escargot. See SNAIL.

Escarole (*chicorée scarole*). A smooth-leaved green endive – Batavian endive – as opposed to the curly endive or *chicorée frisée*. Used as a winter salad. See CHICORY.

Espagnole. One of the *sauces mères*, *sauce espagnole* is a rich brown sauce made with a MIREPOIX and a FONDS BRUN. After the *dépouillement* (see DÉPOUILLER) and straining, the sauce is finished by the addition of a little strong tomato pulp and a glass of sherry.

Estouffade. Strong clear broth. (See FONDS BRUN.) Also a beef stew.

Evaporated Milk. See CONDENSED MILK.

Fagot (or Faggot). The English for a BOUQUET GARNI, i.e. a bundle of herbs.

A fagot is also a square of highly seasoned minced meat including liver, sold ready cooked for eating cold or for reheating. In this case, the name is probably a corruption of 'fag-ends'.

Farce (or Forcemeat). STUFFING of various kinds. To farce also means to stuff.

Fat. In culinary terms, fat is generally taken to be animal fat, i.e. lard, mutton, or beef fat. Other fats, for example vegetable, are known as OIL, and include both that from olives and the deodorized oils from nuts and seeds – groundnut, almond, maize, and so on. Fat, in some form, is a most necessary ingredient in cookery, food being dull and tasteless and containing little nourishment without it. See BUTTER, CREAM, MARGARINE, SUET.

Fécule (French for starch). In cookery, a fine starch, potato flour or arrowroot.

Fennel. There are two species of fennel. The first, *Foeniculum vulgare*, is a perennial feathery herb easily grown in our gardens and used sparingly in sauces for fish. *Foeniculum dulce* (Florence fennel or finocchio) is an annual grown in Italy or the south of France where there is enough sun to ripen the white bulbous root. This is eaten raw and sliced in a salad, or cooked and quartered as a vegetable. It has a strong flavour of aniseed when raw, but a more delicate flavour when cooked. See CRUDITÉS.

Fenugreek (*Trigonella*). A spice, usually included as one of the ingredients of curry powder.

Fermière. A method of preparing pot-roasted or braised meat with a garnish of root vegetables, cooked either with the meat or separately in butter.

Fettucine. Ribbon-like PASTA.

Feuilleton. See FLEURON.

Fig. Dried, pressed figs, which are soaked before stewing, are the most commonly known in England, but small wooden boxes of specially selected dried dessert figs come into the shops in late November for the Christmas market. Fresh figs, the round black variety, are imported from the Mediterranean during the late summer. The oval green fig is seldom seen in England except from a private garden or cool greenhouse.

Filbert (*Corylus maxima*). (Also called cob-nut.) A big oval nut with an outer husk, sold for dessert. The kernels can also be used in the same way as HAZELNUTS.

Fillet. (1) The undercut of a sirloin of beef.

(2) In fish, the flesh which lies on either side of the back-bone. In small flat fish (sole, plaice, etc.) the flesh may be cut from the bone in one piece from the top or under side (a double fillet), or in two pieces so giving four fillets for each fish. In larger flat fish, e.g. turbot or halibut, the fish is cut into steaks rather than fillets. Round fish (cod, haddock, etc.) may be cut into fillets or steaks.

(3) In chicken the white meat of breast and wing together may be called a fillet (see SUPRÊME), especially the smaller piece lying next to the bone (*filet mignon*).

Financière. A name given to a garnish for poultry and meat dishes which, as the name implies, is an expensive one, and is a mixture of truffles, cocks' combs, olives and mushrooms.

Fines Herbes. Mixed herbs such as parsley, thyme, marjoram, chives, etc., chopped and added to omelets, butter, farces, etc. Nowadays this term is generally used simply of chopped parsley.

Finnan Haddock. See HADDOCK.

Flageolet. See BEAN.

Flaky Pastry. See PASTRY.

Flamber. To flame food (usually meat or game) with a spirit, e.g. brandy, or a fortified wine, e.g. sherry, in order to give flavour and at the same time to reduce the alcohol content of the spirit or wine. The brandy or sherry is heated to make the spirit volatile, set alight, and then poured flaming over the food, which is first partially, or in some cases wholly, cooked.

Flan. A shallow pastry (generally short-crust) case filled with fruit either before or after baking, depending on the kind of fruit. Stone fruit, e.g. plums, apples, etc., may be cooked in the pastry, while strawberries or raspberries are best arranged in a previously baked flan-case. Savoury flans are made with a cheese, fish, or meat filling.

Flapjack. A mixture of rolled oats, brown sugar and melted butter pressed into a shallow tin and baked. It is cut into squares or fingers while still warm.

Fleuron. Small crescent-shaped pieces of puff pastry used to garnish fish which is dished coated with a rich sauce. They are made by rolling out trimmings of puff pastry very thinly, brushing the surface with beaten egg and cutting crescents from this with a round fluted cutter $2\frac{1}{2}$ to 3 inches in diameter. Bake the fleurons in a hot oven for 7 to 10 minutes.

Flitch. A side of bacon. Pigs destined for bacon are split down the back, the chine bone removed and also the hind legs (hams). The fore legs and shoulders are usually taken off too, though in small pigs these may be left on. See BACON.

Florentine. (1) Accompanied by or garnished with spinach, either in leaf form or a purée.

(2) Florentines are wafer-thin biscuits containing nuts and dried fruits and coated with melted chocolate. The distinguishing feature is that the chocolate is spread with a comb giving it a wavy line.

(3) In the past a florentine was a pie with a fruit filling covered with a flaky or puff paste, well ornamented with leaves and scrolls of the paste and cooked in a shallow dish.

Flounder. A somewhat bony flat fish, but sweet and good when freshly caught. It should not be confused with plaice though in some parts of England it is so called. In colour it is light brown on the top side with a paler brown or creamy white on the other. Flounder like a shallow sandy bottom and are common round English shores. See DAB.

Flour. The ground or milled grain of cereals, generally rye or wheat. For culinary purposes wheat is the most commonly used and is the main ingredient of our daily bread. There are several grades of wheat flour from the fine white to the coarse wholemeal; the latter is now considered the most nutritious as little is taken out by the milling. In white flour bran, the outer husk of the grain, an important roughage, is removed entirely. Various grades of flour, some containing a proportion of bran, can be bought from those mills which grind by stone rather than the modern method of steel rollers. For *potato flour* see FÉCULE.

Fluid Ounce. See MEASURES.

Flummery. A kind of oatmeal jelly of Welsh origin, sweetened, enriched with cream, and flavoured with sherry.

Foie Gras. The liver of a goose specially fattened by forced feeding. These livers reach an enormous size, around 3–4 lb., and are made principally into *pâtés* and terrines. Strasbourg, Toulouse, and Périgueux are famed for them. See TRUFFLE.

Foil. See ALUMINIUM FOIL.

Fondant. A syrup of sugar and water boiled to 238–240° F. and then worked until white and solid. A long wooden spatula is used at first to work the syrup on a flat surface, and when stiff and white it is kneaded by hand until smooth. Fondant is used as a centre for chocolate creams, or warmed and diluted with a thick syrup for cake icing. In both cases flavours are added to taste. A fondant powder is now available for dilution for icing, which cuts out considerable labour.

Fonds Blanc and **Fonds Brun**. Stock, either white (*blanc*) or brown (*brun*). To prepare *fonds blanc*, white meat and bones (e.g. veal) are blanched and then simmered gently in water with vegetables to flavour. Used for blanquettes, suprêmes, velouté soups, etc. For a *fonds brun* the bones may be beef (and/or veal) but are browned first in a little fat before the addition of liquid. The vegetables are also browned. *Fonds brun* is used for *demi-glace*, ragouts, braises, etc. See STOCK.

Fondue. A cheese cream, which originated in Switzerland. It consists of cheese, usually Gruyère or Emmenthal, melted in white wine, and seasoned with pepper and a little Kirsch. Special dishes or casseroles are sold for a fondue, which should ideally be made at the table. Each guest dips a piece of bread held on a fork into the melted cheese, and eats it piping hot.

Fondue bourguignonne, a dish which has recently become fashionable, is served and eaten in the same way, with the exception that, in place of cheese, the main ingredient is tender fillet steak cut into squares. The centre dish is metal and holds smoking hot oil, and each guest spears a piece of meat on a long fork and fries it for two or three minutes. Before being eaten the meat is dipped into small bowls of spiced sauces arranged round the centre dish.

Certain vegetables cooked for a long time in butter until they are reduced to a purée are also called *fondue*.

Fool. A purée of fruit either raw, e.g. strawberry, or cooked, e.g. gooseberry. The purée is sweetened to taste and mixed with approximately half its volume of partially whipped cream. A fool may be served in individual glasses with a sweet biscuit.

Forcemeat. See STUFFING.

Fowl. A generic term for chickens of whatever age, whether cocks or hen birds. It is, however, customary to call an old hen a 'boiling fowl'.

71

Frangipane. Either an almond-flavoured pastry cream, or a rich cake mixture made with a large proportion of ground almonds. This mixture is frequently used in the making of *gâteaux* and *pâtisseries*.

Frankfurter. A German sausage made of finely minced pork and lightly smoked. Frankfurters are light brown in colour, rather thin, and about 4 inches in length, and are cooked by being poached in boiling water for 5–7 minutes, or broiled under a hot grill. They are the sausages used for hot dogs, and are also eaten with CHOUCROUTE.

Frappé. French for iced, applies particularly to liquids, fruit sweets, and creams.

Freezer. A machine for making ices. The best is the churn-type freezer, consisting of a wooden bucket with a metal container and dasher. These are held with a bar and ratchet across the top and a handle to turn the dasher. The space between the bucket and the container is filled with a mixture of broken ice and coarse (i.e. freezing) salt. Freezers are obtainable at most big stores or ironmongers and with care will last for years. See also ICES.

French Dressing. A salad dressing of 3–4 parts of olive oil and 1 part wine vinegar or lemon juice, seasoned with salt, freshly ground pepper, and sometimes mustard. The mixture is well stirred or shaken before use.

Fricadelle. Minced meat, either raw or cooked, shaped into small balls and fried. May be finished with a sauce or left plain.

Fricandeau. A long piece from the fillet of veal. The meat should be butchered in the French manner in order to get this cut from the leg. Traditionally a *fricandeau* is braised and served with various garnishes; the best known is perhaps *fricandeau à l'oseille*, in which the *fricandeau* is served with a purée of sorrel.

Fricassée. A *réchauffé* dish with a white sauce. Fricassée of chicken: neatly cut pieces of cooked chicken warmed through in a creamy *béchamel* sauce and served with boiled rice. Creamed chicken, or chicken à la King, is also a fricassée.

Fritter. Any piece of food dipped into fritter batter and fried in deep fat. The best known are apple or banana fritters, made with raw fruit. Cooked meat bound with a sauce is usually divided into small portions, and each wrapped in bacon before being dipped in batter. See KROMESKI and BEIGNET.

Frog. The green or edible frog (*Rana esculenta*) found in Europe is considered a delicacy, especially in France. Though not indigenous to England it was imported into eastern and southern counties in the last century. The back and legs of the frog are the only part eaten, and they may be grilled, fried, or served in a fricassée. The meat is tender and slightly gelatinous. Frogs are also esteemed as a delicacy in the U.S., though there a different variety is caught.

Frosting. See ICING.

Frumenty. An old English country dish made from creed or stewed wheat. To cree the wheat the whole grain is first well soaked in cold water and then cooked slowly until tender. To this jelly-like porridge, milk and sometimes egg-yolks and cream are added, according to the part of the country where the frumenty is made. At one time honey and spices were used to sweeten and flavour. Frumenty can be eaten as a breakfast cereal and in its richer form as a sweet. It is considered very wholesome and a source of vitamins A and B.

Frying. An important cooking process and one which can be divided into three categories: (1) dry frying; (2) shallow frying; (3) deep-fat frying.

(1) DRY FRYING
Used essentially for cooking steaks, cutlets, or chops and when well done gives the result of a good grill. The frying-pan should be thick, and the amount of fat very small, barely enough to cover the bottom of the pan. The pan should be very hot before the meat is put in, and the subsequent cooking done on full heat.

(2) SHALLOW FRYING

Used for eggs, fish, fishcakes, croûtes, etc. Here the fat is between $\frac{1}{4}$ and $\frac{3}{4}$ in. deep in the pan, depending on what is to be fried. For example, for a cutlet coated with egg and crumbs the fat must come half-way up the side of the meat so that when it is turned the side is evenly browned and leaves no 'white line'.

(3) DEEP-FAT FRYING

The food is totally immersed in the hot fat. All foods cooked by this method should have a protective coating of some kind (egg and breadcrumbs, batter, or flour) to prevent the juices getting into the fat. After use the fat is carefully strained off and kept for future use. The temperature of fat varies a little but in general should be smoking, i.e. at haze point, otherwise the food is greasy. The exception is when dough or pastry is fried: here the fat should be barely at haze point to allow the food to cook before browning. This exception applies also to potatoes, which are then fried a second time in smoking hot fat to brown and crisp. All fried food should be drained on a wire rack or absorbent paper.

Fudge. A sugary sweetmeat. A thick syrup made with sugar, water or milk, and a little butter, and flavoured with chocolate or vanilla, etc. The syrup is boiled to about 240° F. (when it forms a soft ball when dropped into cold water), and then beaten to a thick cream which results in a fine graining. The mixture is then poured off into a shallow tin and cut into squares when cold.

Fumet. The essence of fish, meat, or game. Nowadays the term is generally applied to strong, well-reduced fish stock.

G

Galantine. A dish for the cold table. A galantine may be of either boned chicken or breast of veal, stuffed with a meat farce, rolled tightly in a cloth, and simmered until tender. After being lightly pressed it is finished with a *chaudfroid* or meat glaze and suitably decorated. A galantine may also consist of forcemeat only, shaped into a roll and cooked and finished as above. Galantines may also be braised instead of being cooked in water.

Galette. French for a round flat cake made of flaky pastry. The best known is perhaps the *galette des rois*, a rich yeast pastry cake made for Epiphany or Twelfth Night. A large bean is hidden in the galette and the finder becomes king for the evening.

Game. Any wild bird or animal shot for gastronomic reasons and classed as sport comes under this heading. All game, with the exception of pigeon and rabbit, is protected by law and has a closed season when it may not be shot or sold.

The open seasons vary and are: Black Game – 20 August to 10 December; Capercailzie – 20 August to 10 December; Grouse – 12 August to 10 December; Hare – September–October to 28 January; Partridge – 1 September to 1 February; Pheasant – 1 October to 1 February; Snipe – 1 September to 28 February; Teal – 1 September to 28 February; Widgeon – 1 September to 28 February; Wild Duck – 1 September to 28 February; Woodcock – 1 September to 28 February; Venison – late June to January (red, roe, and fallow deer); Buck venison – late June to late September; Doe venison remains in season through November and December.

Game Chip. See CHIP.

Gammon. The cured leg of a pig, usually the fore leg, the hind legs being reserved for hams. Gammon may be smoked or unsmoked (green). See also BACON.

Garbure. A thick soup or vegetable purée native to the Béarnais region of France.

Garlic (*Allium sativum*). A pungent root much used in the kitchen. When dried (as an onion is treated) the root is white and is divided into 6–8 sections, called cloves. Garlic is considered wholesome but care must be taken to use it sparingly as too much can kill the flavour of a dish.

Garnish. To trim or to decorate a dish. A good garnish is of real importance in cooking, adding to both the flavour and the appearance of the dish. The name of the dish may also denote the garnish: e.g. *parisienne*, with cream sauce and mushrooms, from the little white button mushrooms known as *champignons de Paris*.

Gaspacho. A highly flavoured Spanish soup of onion, tomatoes, garlic, and cucumber. It is sometimes thickened with the crumb of white bread soaked in olive oil, and usually served ice cold.

Gâteau (French for cake). In England *gâteau* usually denotes a rich iced cake or one filled with cream and served as a sweet.

Gaufre. See WAFFLE.

Gaufrette (French for wafer). So called after the gauffering iron used for stamping patterns on velvet.

Gefilte Fish. See CARP.

Gelatine. A substance derived from the bones or tissues of animals or fish by prolonged boiling. It is used to set liquids, e.g. jellies, cream sweets, etc. A good quality gelatine, either in leaf or now more commonly in powder form, should always be used. Proportions for setting are given in every recipe containing gelatine. See ISINGLASS.

Genoese. A whisked sponge mixture of eggs and sugar to which when thick very soft creamed butter is added with the flour. There are two types of Genoese, *fin* and *commune*, the former containing more butter than the latter. Both are widely used in French and Continental *pâtisserie*. English Genoese is made by creaming the butter, beating in the sugar and then the eggs and flour. Victoria sponge is a type of Genoese.

Ghee. Butter made from buffalo milk, which is clarified by boiling so that it resembles oil in consistency. It is frequently used for frying in Indian cookery.

Gherkin. A very small cucumber grown specially for pickling and preserved in vinegar; the best are not more than about 1½ in. long. They are used mostly for garnishes and cocktail savouries.

Gibelotte. A savoury stew of rabbit, bacon, and onions.

Giblets. Those parts of the insides (or viscera) of poultry which are edible, i.e. the neck, heart, gizzard, and liver. To these may be added the feet. Certain of the giblets, the neck, gizzard, and feet especially, make excellent stock for gravy, and also a good soup. The gizzard must first be opened and the thick membrane containing grit peeled off, and the feet scalded to remove the outer skin. The gall bladder on the liver should be carefully cut away without being broken and the liver itself used for savouries and stuffings. All giblets should be well washed before use with the exception of the liver.

Gigot. French for a leg of lamb or mutton. The word is also common in Scotland for the same joint.

Gill. See MEASURES.

Gin. A spirit distilled from grain, and flavoured with juniper berries. The word gin is a corruption of *genièvre*, the French for juniper. At one time gin was manufactured almost exclusively in Holland, and was known as Hollands or Geneva. The London distilleries became famous soon after, and now gin is made all over the world. Good gin has a smooth dry flavour; it is now drunk chiefly as an apéritif, and is the base of many cocktails.

Sloe or damson gin, an infusion of the berries in gin with sugar, can be made at home. It may be drunk as a liqueur or a warming mid-morning 'tot' in winter.

Ginger. The rhizome of the ginger plant, the dried white or Jamaican ginger being considered the best. It is used for infusion with pickling spices, or grated to flavour chutneys, curries, or sauces. Green ginger, i.e. the fresh root, is imported at certain times of the year and can be bought in shops specializing in oriental provisions. Crystallized ginger for use in cakes, and ginger preserved in syrup (stem ginger) for a dessert, are the best and most expensive forms.

Gingerbread. The old name for ginger cake, still used in many North Country districts.

Girdle. See GRIDDLE.

Glacé (French for glazed). A term applied to sugar icing, e.g. glacé icing, and *fruits glacés*, fruit dipped into a syrup boiled to the crack (see SYRUP) which when cold hardens. Glacé also implies iced, e.g. *bombe glacée*, iced bombe.

Glaze. Meat glaze is strong gravy or bone stock reduced by being boiled to a brown syrup, which when cold sets hard and firm. A small nut of this may be added to a gravy or brown sauce to strengthen the flavour. Glaze may also be melted down and used for brushing over galantines, cold tongues, etc. As meat glaze is difficult to make for the small household in these days, owing to the large quantity of good stock required for a very small quantity of glaze, a mock one can be made with a good clear brown stock stiffened with gelatine. Brush this over the meat when on the point of setting. Jam glaze, from apricot jam or red-currant jelly, is used for brushing over fruit flans, cakes, etc.

To glaze means to make shiny with either egg, water and sugar, or the above glazes.

Globe Artichoke. See ARTICHOKE.

Glucose. Grape sugar or dextrose, commercially prepared from carbohydrates. Powdered glucose is used medicinally, while that for culinary use is a thick clear syrup (the American corn syrup) and is manufactured either from maize or by the hydrolysis of any starch. Liquid glucose is of value in confectionery because it does not crystallize, and so when added to a sugar syrup will prevent it from graining, i.e. crystallizing, as it boils.

Gluten. A sticky substance found in the grain of wheat which gives tenacity to flour. By certain processes the gluten content of flour can be altered; for example flour with a high gluten content (known as springs) is used by bakers for bread-making.

Glycerine. Used in the commercial manufacture of cakes to keep them moist; also added to royal icing for easy working.

Gnocchi. There are three distinct types of gnocchi: (1) Italian, made with *polenta* (maize meal) or semolina cooked in water and flavoured with cheese; (2) potato gnocchi; and (3) French gnocchi, made with chou paste and flavoured with cheese. Italian and French gnocchi are finished with a sauce; potato gnocchi usually with melted butter and served to accompany a meat dish.

Goose. Once called the kings of poultry, geese have been famous over the centuries. Roast goose was the traditional fare for Christmas before the advent of the turkey. As well as celebrating the feast of St Michael, the Michaelmas goose was also a harvest thanksgiving; the young geese were fattened on the corn stubble and so were at their prime by Michaelmas. Traditionally roast goose is stuffed with sage and onion and served with apple sauce.

Gooseberry. A summer fruit. The first gooseberries should by tradition appear in a pie on the table on Whitsunday, but this is sometimes difficult to accomplish as Whitsun is a movable feast. Gooseberries are at their best when poached in syrup flavoured with elderflower and served ice-cold with thick cream. Excellent for fools, jam, or jelly.

Gorgonzola. An Italian blue cheese.

Goujon. See GUDGEON.

Goulash (Gulyas). A highly seasoned stew of beef, lamb, or veal, with a large quantity of onions. Goulash may also be flavoured with sweet pepper (paprika goulash). The dish is of Hungarian origin.

Graham Flour or Bread. The American equivalent of coarse wholemeal, named after an American dietitian. The English counterpart is the GRANT LOAF.

Graining. A term connected with sugar-boiling. Refined sugar when heated beyond 245–250° F. will grain or candy, i.e. form small crystals after agitation. To prevent (or to retard) this crystallization a small quantity of liquid glucose or cream of tartar is added to the syrup; this is known as 'cutting the grain'.

Grant or Granary Loaf. Doris Grant some years ago compiled an easy and simple recipe for making a coarse wholemeal bread at home. Flour, yeast, and liquid are mixed together, turned straight into baking-tins, and left to rise. The loaves are then baked. This method cuts out the sponging and proving which form part of the normal process of bread-making. See BREAD.

Grape. The fruit of the vine. Grown in England under glass, grapes are widely cultivated in Europe and other countries, chiefly for wine-making. Different varieties are grown for dessert, for wine-making, and for drying, i.e. for currants, sultanas, and raisins. With imports from various countries grapes, both black and white, are available throughout the year at reasonable prices.

Grapefruit. A large juicy citrus fruit (an improved variety of the shaddock). The thin-skinned fruit are often the juiciest, and the quality may be judged by their relative weight.

Gratin, Au Gratin, and **Gratiner.** To brown with crumbs, butter, and sometimes cheese. To cook fish *au gratin*, the raw fish is laid in a dish and coated with a thick white sauce or *béchamel*; the surface is finished with a scattering of browned crumbs, melted butter, and/or grated cheese. The whole is then baked in the oven for 20–25 minutes. While it is cooking, the juices from the fish run into the sauce and so bring it to a 'flowing' consistency. Cooked food, such as a vegetable (e.g. cauliflower *au gratin*) or eggs, is coated with a cheese sauce and browned quickly in the oven. Prolonged cooking of a cheese sauce would cause it to curdle. A *gratin* dish is of fireproof material and frequently has 'ears', i.e. protuberances at both ends for easy handling when it is taken from the oven.

Gravy. The juices from roasting meat. These (being heavier than fat) form a sediment on the bottom of the tin and once the fat has been poured off are diluted with a little strong stock. Additional colour may be given by frying a slice of onion in a tablespoon of the dripping in the tin. Gravy may also be thickened, depending on the type of roast, but this is only so that more liquid can be added to increase the quantity.

Grayling. A fish caught in fresh water and very similar in size and appearance to trout. Grayling are rarely seen except by fishermen.

Greengage. A variety of plum, round and slightly flattened at the stalk end. The colour is a dark green with the flesh turning to gold as it ripens, and the flavour scented and honey sweet. The greengage should not be confused with a yellow plum sometimes called the greengage plum. The true gage can be distinguished by the stone, which is round rather than oval like the plum stone.

Grenadin. *Grenadins* are small rounds of veal cut from the leg about ¾–1 in. thick. Prepared and cooked in the same way as a *fricandeau*.

Grey Mullet. See MULLET.

Griddle (or Girdle). A thick round plate of iron with a half-hoop handle over the top. Used for baking soda bread, scones, and oatcakes on the top of the cooker.

Grilling. An important method of cooking by radiant heat. Grilling in the domestic kitchen is done either by electricity or gas, or by charcoal for out-of-door barbecues. The grill may also be used for spit-roasting.

Grilse. A young SALMON that has been down to the sea for the first time and returned to its native river.

Grissini. Long crisp sticks of a rusk-like bread. Usually seen in Italian restaurants, presented in tumblers on each table.

Groats. Oatmeal.

Groundnut Oil. See OIL.

Ground Rice. See RICE.

Grouse. A small, much-prized game bird in season from 12 August to 10 December. (See GAME.) Its natural habitat is the rolling heather moors, rather than the high tops. The tips of the heather form its staple food. Grouse should be moderately well hung and served plainly roast with fried crumbs, plain gravy, and game chip potatoes.

Gruel. A thin porridge made of meal, oats, barley, etc., once popular for invalids and as a workhouse diet.

Gruyère. Hard Swiss cheese made from rich cow's milk. Its chief characteristic is that it is full of large holes; on cutting these should be moist and have, as it is said, a 'tear-drop' in them. *Emmenthal* is very similar to Gruyère but the holes are smaller. Gruyère is a rich cheese and much prized in the kitchen, either for a fondue or, ideally, mixed with an equal quantity of Parmesan and used in a Mornay sauce or as a finish to a *gratin*. The rich, creamy flavour of the Gruyère contrasts admirably with the spiciness of the Parmesan.

Guava. A tropical fruit about the size of a small apple, with a yellow rind and red pulpy flesh. The flavour is pleasantly acid and makes excellent jelly. The fruit is imported both fresh and canned into England.

Gudgeon. A small fresh-water fish seldom caught nowadays. It may be cooked like whitebait. The French term *en goujons*, i.e. small fried strips of plaice or sole, is derived from this fish's name.

Guinea Fowl. A bird the size of a large pheasant, with flesh of much the same flavour. It is, however, a domestic fowl and can be reared like other poultry. The plumage is dark grey with white spots, and the flesh slightly darker than that of chicken. The guinea fowl comes from Africa and was introduced into England about 1530 when it was known as the 'turkie-henne'.

Gull's Egg. Gull's eggs have become a replacement for plover's eggs since it became illegal to take the latter. They are similar to, though perhaps not so delicate in flavour as, the plover's. The season is very short, about three weeks in late April or early May. Gull's eggs are bought ready hard-boiled from fishmongers and are served in the shell in a napkin as a first course. The accompaniments are brown bread and butter and rock salt from the mill or grinder.

Gulyas. See GOULASH.

Gurnet. A spiny, bony fish with a large head. Gurnet, like mullet, are red or grey and are found off the Cornish coast.

Hachis. A chopped or minced mixture of meat, herbs, etc., generally used for a forcemeat.

Haddock. One of the best white fish. A round fish ranging in weight from 1½ to 5 or 6 lb., with a grey skin easily distinguishable by the black line running down each side and a black smudge behind each gill known as St Peter's mark. The flesh is white and firm and lends itself to many ways of cooking: whole, stuffed with herb forcemeat and roasted like meat with a gravy made from the juices in the pan; fried; or with a sauce. Haddock is also popular smoked. It is called Finnan or Findon, from the name of the small village outside Aberdeen where this method of curing originated. The haddocks are slit open and lightly smoked. Smokies, small whole fish, well smoked, are sold chiefly in Scotland and are equally good.

Haggis. A Scots national dish cooked in the paunch of a sheep. The haggis is a rich forcemeat of the heart, liver, and tongue mixed with oatmeal. The paunch is used to make small bags to hold the stuffing, and they are boiled gently for 2–3 hours, and then left to get cold. It is at this stage that they are offered for sale in butchers' shops. To serve: simmer a haggis (they average 1–1½ lb. each) for about one hour. Then set on a napkin and serve very hot, traditionally with mashed turnips and boiled potatoes. Haggis is not the most decorative of dishes but makes an excellent meal for a cold day. The skin should be slit with a knife and the contents scooped out with a spoon.

Hake. A popular white fish. In size and appearance it resembles cod but has a rough grey skin. The flesh is friable and white and so is suitable for creams and mousses. Hake is caught chiefly off the south-western coasts of England.

Halibut. An enormous flat fish which may weigh up to 100 lb. The flesh is white, firm, and somewhat coarse. Halibut is greatly valued as food, although it does not have the delicate flavour of TURBOT. It is usually bought by the piece for boiling or in steaks for grilling.

Halva (Middle Eastern and Indian cookery). A sweetmeat made with ground sesame seeds (sometimes semolina), sugar, butter, and nuts and flavoured with rose water, saffron, etc.

Ham. The hind leg of a bacon pig specially cured and smoked. There are several varieties of ham; perhaps the most famous and highly prized in England is the York ham. This is a large ham with a very delicate flavour and is only cured and not smoked. Other special cures are Bradenhams (Norfolk), and imported Virginia hams. Smaller smoked hams around 10–12 lb., Irish or Danish, known as breakfast hams, are excellent and less expensive than the special cures. Continental hams such as Bayonne, Prague and the well-known Parma ham are eaten raw and very thinly sliced. See BACON.

Hamburger. Individual meat cakes, formed of raw finely minced beef and dry pan fried. Usually served with fried onion.

Hare. Classed as game. In season from September to the end of January. There are two varieties of hare, the brown, considered the best, and the blue or mountain hare. A young hare (or leveret) shot at the beginning of the season is best for a sauté or for roasting, while an old hare is ideal for jugging, i.e. long slow cooking in wine or stock. Hare, like most game, should be well hung; the paunch or insides should be removed after 4 or 5 days, and the hare can then be hung for a further 3 or 4 days depending on the weather. When paunching a hare, care should be taken not to break the membrane (diaphragm) lying across the lower end of the rib cage. After all the insides have been removed, the membrane may be broken and the blood which lies behind it released and carefully collected. This is used to thicken the gravy or sauce, e.g. for a *civet*, before serving the hare. A poulterer will send the blood with the hare if it is asked for.

Haricot. A dried white BEAN which can be large or small. They are in fact the beans of the runner and kidney or French bean.

A haricot is also a brown mutton stew with onion and carrots. See NAVARIN.

Hâtelet. See ATTELETTE.

Hazelnut. A small round nut, the fruit of the hazel tree (*Corylus avellana*). These nuts are generally sold as kernels and are used in cakes and confectionery. They should be lightly baked or toasted before use, which enables the skins to be rubbed off before the nuts are ground or used whole. Hazelnuts are sometimes called *Barcelona nuts*.

Heart. The most palatable heart is the sheep's. It makes an excellent dish when stuffed with a herb forcemeat, braised, and served with a rich brown gravy.

Herbs. A large variety of plants, mostly aromatic, some of which are of value in the kitchen for flavouring. Care must be taken when using herbs as the majority are strong in flavour. Moreover, some herbs marry better with certain foods than others. The most important herbs in the kitchen are: BASIL, BAY, CHIVES, DILL, FENNEL, MARJORAM, MINT, PARSLEY, ROSEMARY, SAVORY, and TARRAGON. See also FINES HERBES.

Herring. A silvery fish 7–10 in. long caught off English shores. The herring shoals move around the coast, starting in the northwest in April or May, and reach the east coast at Great Yarmouth by October. The fresh fish should be eaten immediately they are caught, as the flesh, being delicate, quickly deteriorates and becomes oily. Lightly salted and smoked and left whole, they are bloaters, a speciality of the east coast, particularly Great Yarmouth. Split open, they are kippered or smoked; this industry is carried out in Scotland.

Hip. The fruit of the wild or dog rose (*Rosa canina*). The best culinary use of hips is in a syrup or jelly, as they contain a quantity of vitamin C. As they are low in pectin a proportion of apple should be added when making jelly. This jelly is a pleasant alternative to red-currant for serving with meat or game.

Hock. Hock is a white German wine. The name was derived originally from the town of Hochheim-on-Main, but has now come loosely to designate all Rhine wines. The wine is sold in tall elegant brown bottles.

Hollandaise. A name given to a sauce, i.e. Holland or Dutch sauce, and also to a way of cooking (*à la hollandaise*). Hollandaise sauce is a rich butter and egg sauce served with fish or vegetables.

Hominy. Ground maize, a meal with the consistency of coarse semolina. Once popular in England for making cream sweets, croquettes, etc.

Homogenize. To emulsify a liquid. Usually applied to milk where the fat globules are held in suspension in the liquid.

Honey. A natural sugar from bees, honey is the earliest form of sweetening. It can be adulterated with other substances, so care should be taken to buy pure honey direct from beekeepers, or one that is guaranteed to be so. Honey may be thick, i.e. with a certain proportion of wax left in it, or clear. It is also obtainable in the comb. The flavour depends on where the bees have been feeding (heather, clover, lime, etc.).

Hors-d'œuvre. A collection of piquant salads or small dishes served as a preliminary to a meal, usually to a lunch rather than a dinner (when soup is normally served). They are designed to whet the appetite, so if three or four *hors-d'œuvres* are arranged on a plate for individual serving they should be light and delicate. *Hors-d'œuvres* may be hot or cold; hot *hors-d'œuvres* were generally served as part of a dinner menu, and cold ones with lunch. However, the two may be served at the same time. A typical selection of *hors-d'œuvres* is: Russian salad, anchovy fillets, salami, egg mayonnaise, spiced fish, tomato salad, spring vegetables.

Horseradish. The hot astringent root of *Cochlearia armoracia* used grated as a condiment. The classic method is to mix it with lightly whipped cream, i.e. horseradish sauce, for serving with roast beef. Horseradish may also be grated over a dish of cold beef or on beetroot salad.

Hot Cross Bun. A yeast bun, with currants and sometimes candied peel. It is marked with a cross and is traditionally made for Good Friday.

Hot Dog (American). A frankfurter sausage broiled or boiled and put inside a soft bread roll. It is served hot.

Hot-Pot. A stew cooked in an earthenware dish topped with potatoes. This dish is indigenous to the Midlands and north of England. The most famous is the Lancashire hot-pot, layers of meat with mushrooms and oysters and a thick layer of potatoes on top. A hot-pot dish is seldom seen nowadays, but is a white earthenware casserole without a lid so allowing the potatoes to brown well during the cooking. Some of these dishes had 'Hot Pot' inscribed on them.

Hurt. See BILBERRY.

Iberian Moss. See CARRAGEEN.

Ices. A sweetened liquid frozen to a firm mass while being churned in a special machine known as an ice-cream FREEZER. The liquid may be a light, flavoured syrup, such as lemon or orange, or a mixture of egg-yolks and cream, or custard flavoured in various ways. The proportion of sugar in the liquid must be just right, as too sweet a mixture will not freeze, and too little sugar gives a hard rocky consistency lacking in flavour. The correct proportion is always given in the recipe. Though the mixture can be frozen in the ice trays of a refrigerator it is not possible to get the light, smooth texture which is the result of churning while freezing.

Icing. A sugar coating to finish and decorate cakes. There are five different sorts of icing:

BUTTER ICING

A simple creamed mixture of butter and icing sugar used for filling plain cakes. It may be flavoured with coffee, chocolate, orange, etc.

FONDANT

Icing of a soft velvety texture, made with a thick syrup boiled to 240° F. and worked until white and smooth. This is then diluted with a stock syrup to the consistency of cream and flavoured as desired. The icing is warmed slightly before use. Light cakes, e.g. GENOESE, are iced with fondant.

FROSTING

An American term for a cake icing. It is made of egg-white and sugar; these are either whisked together over heat, or the sugar is made into a syrup and boiled to 240° F. before being poured on to whisked egg-whites. The whole is then beaten together until firm enough to be spread on to the cake. A frosting should be crisp yet soft.

GLACÉ

Icing sugar worked to a thick cream with a stock syrup or water flavoured as wished before warming. If made with syrup, it is a good imitation of a fondant.

ROYAL

A hard white icing made with egg-white and icing sugar, used for wedding and birthday cakes. A small quantity may be spread and baked on top of certain *pâtisseries* to give a crisp finish.

Icing Sugar. See SUGAR.

Indian Corn. Commonly called green or sweet corn, especially when eaten on the cob. Indian corn is a handsome plant, with broad green pointed leaves, and grows 5–6 ft in height. The cobs are 6–8 in. long, covered with a pale green husk with a silvery plume of fibres at the top. When eaten as green corn the kernels should be soft and milky. Maize, polenta, hominy, and corn-flour are prepared from the dried kernels.

Ink Fish. See OCTOPUS.

Irish Stew. A white stew of mutton, onion, and potatoes. During long slow cooking the potatoes break and thicken the gravy slightly.

Isinglass. An especially fine gelatine made from the dried bladders of fish, particularly that of sturgeon. Isinglass is used in cookery when milk and meat products may not be used together on religious grounds.

Jam. A confection of sugar and fresh fruit boiled together until set. The setting power of any particular jam depends on the PECTIN content of the fruit. In jam the fruit is generally crushed or pulped during cooking; in a conserve the whole fruit is preserved in a heavy syrup.

Jamaican Pepper. See ALLSPICE.

Jardinière, à la. A garnish of fresh vegetables – carrots, turnips, peas, beans, etc. The vegetables may be diced or cut into shapes with a vegetable scoop. They are cooked and served separately round the dish to be garnished.

Jelly. A clear or semi-clear liquid set with gelatine or with a strong gelatinous stock. Calf's foot jelly is an example of the latter. A strong jellied stock is made from calf's feet, well flavoured with lemon and orange, sweetened to taste, and then clarified. Other sweet jellies flavoured with fruit juices or wine and set with gelatine may be clarified or left plain.

ASPIC, a savoury jelly, is best made with a jellied stock so that, although gelatine may have to be used to strengthen the set, the flavour of the aspic will be improved. Aspic is always clarified.

A different type of jelly for use as a preserve is made from the extracted juice of fruit, e.g. red-currant jelly. To the fruit juice, an equal proportion of sugar is added, and the whole boiled until setting point is reached.

Jelly Bag. A bag made of a coarse woollen cloth or felt used in clarifying jellies. Stands are also available on which the bags may be hung.

Jersey Wonder. A speciality of the island of Jersey. Wonders are made from a rich dough of flour, butter, and eggs, formed into small knots, and fried in deep fat until golden-brown. They are best served hot with a fruit sauce.

Jerusalem Artichoke. See ARTICHOKE.

John Dory. An ugly flat fish of small to medium size caught mostly off the south-western shores of England. The flesh is white and firm and has a delicate flavour. The head is very large for its size, and so it does not make a very economical buy.

Juggery. An Indian confection or sweet. An anglicized version is made from tapioca stewed in water or the milk of a coconut until really soft. A spoonful or two of black treacle is added and the sweet is served cold with cream and grated fresh coconut.

Julienne. A garnish of vegetables cut into shreds about 1½ in. long. It is also the name given to a clear vegetable soup made from consommé to which a mixture of finely shredded vegetables is added. The term is also applied to the method of cutting.

Jumble. A BRANDY SNAP or a thin wafer biscuit, curled or rolled.

Juniper. A small fir-like shrub with blue berries. These have a pungent spicy taste and are used fresh or dried in marinades for game. They are also used in the distillation of gin.

Junket. Milk set to a curd with rennet.

Jus. A French term for GRAVY or juices from meat, or fruit.

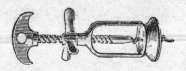

Kabab (or Kebab). Small pieces of meat, generally lamb, grilled or roasted on long skewers. The pieces are interspersed with slices of onion and bay leaves.

Kale. A green winter vegetable of the *Brassica* family, with crisply curled leaves. It is cooked in the same way as cabbage.

Kangaroo. The tail of the kangaroo or wallaby is made into soup. Kangaroo tail soup may be bought in tins.

Kebab. See KABAB.

Kedgeree. An anglicized Indian dish of rice and fish mixed together. Sometimes eggs and cream are added to moisten the mixture.

Ketchup. A spicy bottled sauce, e.g. mushroom ketchup, the juice of mushrooms steeped in vinegar and the liquid then spiced; tomato ketchup, a sauce of puréed tomatoes, spices, and vinegar.

Kid. The young of a goat. If killed under 4 months old, it is a delicacy. Best roasted.

Kidney. Classed as offal. There are four different types:

Lamb's Kidneys. The most prized; usually grilled or sautéd.
Calf's Kidneys. Delicate in flavour; served sautéd or braised, whole or sliced.
Pig's Kidneys. (Same shape as lamb's, but larger.) Rather strong in flavour, but useful for *pâtés* and stuffings.
Ox Kidneys. Strong and often tough, so best cooked with other meat, e.g. steak and kidney pie or pudding.

Kipper. A HERRING that is split open, salted, and smoked.

Kirsch. A liqueur distilled from the fermented juices of wild cherries. One of the best liqueurs for use in the kitchen as it goes well with fruit, especially pineapple. It is also used in cream sweets and soufflés. The finest Kirsch comes from Alsace and the Black Forest.

Kissel. See RÖD GRÖD.

Kneading. An important process in bread-making. Once the flour, water, yeast, etc. have been mixed to form a dough, this is worked on a board or table. To knead, take the edge of the dough, bring it to the centre, and push outwards with the knuckles. This is repeated many times to develop the gluten in the dough. It may also be done in an electric mixer using a bread hook.

Knives. Kitchen knives should be of good steel and kept well cleaned and sharpened. They are all measured by the blade, e.g. a 6-inch chopping knife, and they follow a certain pattern or shape:

Chopping. Useful all-purpose knife. Made in two sizes, large and medium, with a firm blade and a good weight.
Filleting. A thin, slightly springy knife used both for filleting fish and for slicing fillets of chicken, etc.
Fruit. These are of stainless steel, with a serrated edge, also in varying sizes.
Palette. A round-bladed, somewhat flexible knife, made in varying sizes. Palette knives have no cutting edge and are used largely in the kitchen for turning food while cooking, e.g. in shallow fat frying, or for lifting biscuits, etc. from baking-sheets.
Vegetable. Small knives in varying sizes for cutting and shaping vegetables.

Kohlrabi. A turnip-like root with blue-green leaves, similar to those of kale, sprouting from it. The root may be cooked and served in the same way as SWEDE.

Kromeski. A creamed mixture of chicken, game, or veal divided into small pieces and wrapped in thin rashers of bacon. These are then dipped into fritter batter and fried in deep fat. Kromeskies are served as a main course or savoury.

Kulich (Russian). A rich dough similar to a brioche which is baked in tall narrow moulds. The top is iced and decorated with hundreds and thousands. The cake is sliced across in rounds and the top replaced if the whole cake is not all eaten at once. A speciality made for Easter.

Kümmel. A LIQUEUR made from caraway or cummin seeds.

Kumquat. A very small citrus fruit similar to an orange. They are preserved whole in a thick syrup and sold in jars in England.

L

Lactic Acid. The acid of sour milk. See MILK and PASTEURIZE.

Lamb. The young of sheep. When a sheep is 8 months old it becomes mutton.

Lamb's Lettuce. See CORN SALAD.

Lamprey. An eel-like fish which attaches itself to any solid object under water such as wood or stone. Though a sea fish lampreys, like salmon, come into certain rivers in the spring to spawn. Though seldom seen nowadays, in medieval times lampreys were considered a delicacy. Large quantities were caught in the season, from Christmas to June, principally in the River Severn. Though the flesh is soft and gelatinous, it is hard to digest, which may account for the story that a surfeit of lampreys caused the death of Henry I. They may be stewed, made into a pie, or baked.

Langouste. See CRAWFISH.

Langue de Chat (Cat's tongue). A thin, flat, shaped biscuit. In *confiserie* they are made of plain chocolate, in *pâtisserie* a sponge biscuit mixture. When baked *langues de chats* are well browned round the edges and straw coloured in the centre. They are served as *petits fours secs* or with ices.

Lard. The rendered-down fat of a pig. Good lard is pure white and has no smell. It is sometimes flavoured with rosemary. Lard is of value as a shortening and is, after oil, the best frying medium.

Larding. A process carried out to give additional fat to cuts of meat that have little or none of their own, e.g. fillet of veal and fillet of beef. The raw meat is 'sewn' with small pieces of fat (see LARDON) using a larding NEEDLE.

Lardon. Lardons are strips of fat about $1\frac{1}{2}$ in. long and $\frac{1}{4}$ in. wide and thick, cut from a slice of larding bacon. This bacon is specially cured without the use of saltpetre (so that the meat does not discolour) and is solid fat. It is also used for BARDING. Larding bacon is not always easy to obtain, though a Polish variety called spik is usually available at Delicatessens. Pork fat is a good substitute.

Lasagne. These are wide ribbons of PASTA, either green (*lasagne verde*, flavoured with spinach) or plain. The paste can be made at home, like ravioli, and dried lightly before it is boiled. Alternatively it can be bought from most Italian or Delicatessen stores in packets. After it has been boiled lasagne is layered with a meat mixture and coated with a cheese sauce, or more simply with grated cheese and butter before browning in the oven.

Lamb or Mutton

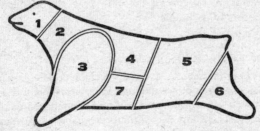

1. Head – *Broths.*
2. Scrag – *Stew.*
3. Shoulder – *Roast or braise.*
4. Neck: Best end – nearest loin – *Cutlets and roast whole*;

middle neck – nearest scrag – *Haricots, stews.*
5. Loin or double loin (saddle) – *Roast or braise.*
6. Leg – *Roast or braise.*
7. Breast – *Stew or braise.*

Laver. Green laver (*Ulva latissima*) and purple laver (*Porphyra laciniata*) are both edible seaweeds and are common round the west coast of Britain and Ireland. When gathered laver is well washed and stewed to a pulp, and then heated with lemon juice, salt and pepper, and a lump of butter, and eaten hot on toast or with meat. Laver may be bought ready prepared in seaside towns in the south-west.

Leek (*Allium porrum*). A handsome and popular vegetable, at its best from November to March. Leeks, like celery, should be grown in trenches to give a good 5 inches of well-blanched stem. The leaves are green and flag-like and the whole plant has a subtle onion flavour. Leeks are delicious both hot and cold. They can be served as a salad with a mayonnaise or vinaigrette dressing.

Lemon. 'A citrus fruit of deep importance in the kitchen', to quote an old cookery book. Both the rind, or zest, and the juice are used to flavour sweet and savoury dishes, sauces, and salad dressings, where the juice is a good replacement for vinegar. The white pith lying between the zest and the flesh is a valuable source of PECTIN, as are the pips. Lemons are imported into England at all seasons of the year from the Mediterranean countries and the Middle East.

Lemon Balm. See BALM.

Lemon Sole. See SOLE.

Lentil (*Lens esculenta*). A dried vegetable resembling a split pea, but smaller and of a different family. The plant is a hardy annual with a feather-shaped leaf and a small pod containing two seeds. There are two varieties available in England, the golden lentil and the brown or German lentil; the former is smaller and cooks more quickly. Lentils should be soaked in water or stock until soft before cooking. They are used for soups and purées and to make the Indian dhal.

Lettuce. To quote from a Victorian cookery book: 'If it were not for lettuces the British cook would almost be at a loss for salad material; whereas the Continental cook would never fail to produce a salad so long as anything of a vegetable character were to hand.' Lettuces are so universal as a salad vegetable that they tend to pall, but people seldom think of cooking them, and in many opinions they are better that way than raw. There are two main varieties of lettuce, the cabbage and the cos. Cabbage lettuces are in season out of doors from April to October (after that they are grown in cool greenhouses) and are at their best in April and May. They are followed by the cos, an upright lettuce with especially crisp leaves. Webbs or iceberg lettuce, also in season during the late summer, is cabbage in shape and has a crisp crinkled leaf.

Leveret. A young HARE.

Liaison. Thickening, a culinary process designed to give body to a liquid food, sauce or broth. Examples of liaisons are a *roux*, which forms the base of a sauce, and egg-yolk and cream, which give a more delicate thickening to a cream soup. There are other liaisons, and these may be found in any good cookery book.

Lights. The lungs of an animal, those of a bullock being most commonly sold. So called, quite literally because of their lightness.

Lima Bean (or Flageolet). See BEAN.

Lime (*Citrus limetta*). A smaller, thin-skinned version of the lemon, not often seen in England. When imported, chiefly from the West Indies, mainly the juice is used for the making of cordials.

Ling. A large species of cod with somewhat coarser flesh. It is usually sold dried and salted. When well soaked it makes a good fish stew, and can also be used for any dish which calls for salt cod.

Liqueur. A name given to alcoholic syrups distilled from wine or brandy and flavoured with fruit, herbs, or spices. There are innumerable liqueurs of varying alcoholic content. Nearly all have secret formulae even though the main ingredient is known. Liqueurs are drunk with the coffee after a meal, in liqueur glasses which seldom contain more than one or two tablespoonfuls. See BENEDICTINE, CHERRY BRANDY, CRÈME DE MENTHE, CURAÇAO, DRAMBUIE, KIRSCH, KÜMMEL, MARASCHINO, NOYAU.

Liver. Classed as offal and considered highly nutritious. Calf's, lamb's, pig's, and ox liver may be bought; the first two have a more delicate flavour. Pig's liver is rather strong for most dishes, but excellent for making a farce, or for terrines. Liver should be eaten very fresh, not hung at all, and is best sliced and fried with a little bacon. Care should be taken not to overcook it as this makes the slices tough and dry. Goose liver, as well as that of other poultry, is well suited for *pâtés*. See CONTINENTAL SAUSAGES.

Lobster. A highly prized shellfish found along rocky shores round English coasts. Rich dark blue in colour when alive it turns scarlet when cooked or boiled. Lobsters lend themselves to both hot and cold dishes. The former, in order to preserve the flavour, should be made with 'live' lobsters, i.e. those killed by piercing the brain immediately before cooking; the latter with freshly boiled lobsters. From the culinary point of view the lobster should be plunged into boiling water and then simmered for the required time. In this way no juices are lost and the flesh is tender and succulent. Both this method and that of piercing the brain are quick and instantaneous ways of killing the lobster. The cock lobster is the one most favoured for its size and is easily distinguished by the brightness of colour and the narrowness of the tail. However, many people prefer the hen lobster, though smaller, for the flavour and tenderness of the flesh. The tail is broader than the cock's, and the coral or roe used for colouring and flavouring sauces, etc. is carried in the tail.

Loganberry. A summer fruit, a cross between a raspberry and a blackberry but more acid than either. Loganberries should be eaten cooked or made into a purée for fools, ice creams, etc.

Loin. That part of an animal which extends from the ribs to the tail. In beef a double loin, i.e. one not split down the chine or backbone, is known as a baron of beef, in lamb or mutton as a saddle.

Lovage (*Levisticum officinale*). A perennial herb with a handsome grey-green serrated leaf, tasting strongly of celery.

Luting Paste. A paste of flour and water used to seal the lid or cover of a terrine to prevent steam escaping when a *pâté* is being cooked.

Lychee. A Chinese fruit about the size of a cherry and growing in bunches in a similar way. The flesh is white, tinged with pink, and of the delicate flavour and texture of muscat grapes. The cover is a thin shell easily removed. Lychees are sold fresh, tinned in syrup, or dried in the shell, when they resemble raisins.

Lyonnais. A dish described as *lyonnais* is named after a famous gastronomic region of France. The district has many specialities, *pâtés*, sausages, *quenelles de brochet*, *gras double lyonnaise*, to name a few. The region is also famed for the quality of its onions and potatoes.

Macaroni. A PASTA made in the form of a tube about $\frac{1}{4}$ inch in diameter or slightly less. It is simmered in water like other pastas, drained when tender, and then mixed with various sauces, cheese perhaps being the best known in England. Macaroni in late Victorian days was popular in a milk pudding, known as 'pipe pudding', one only the English could have invented.

Macaroon. A rich almond biscuit originating from France, those from Nancy being the most famous. Macaroons are round in shape and made solely from pounded or ground almonds mixed with sugar and egg-white.

Mace. Frond-like tendrils covering the outside of the nutmeg. These tendrils may be left whole (blade mace), or ground. Blade mace is used for flavouring spiced vinegars and milk for a *béchamel* sauce; ground mace for vegetable dishes and farces with mixed spice. Mace is considered to have a more delicate flavour than nutmeg. See SPICE.

Macédoine. A mixture of vegetables or fruit. Carrots, turnips, potatoes, etc. are cut into large dice either before or after cooking, and mixed with cooked peas or beans. These may be served hot bound with a cream sauce or cold with a mayonnaise. For a macédoine of fruit, peaches, pears, bananas, etc. are sliced and moistened with a thick syrup.

Macerate (French *macérer*). To soak or infuse in liquid. Usually applied to fresh fruit moistened with brandy, rum, or liqueur, or chopped glacé fruit which is to be added to a cake mixture.

102

Mackerel. A remarkably handsome fish caught round English coasts and in northern waters from May to September. Like that of most fighting fish the flesh is firm and crisp when caught. Mackerel should be eaten as fresh as possible, as after two or three days the flesh tends to become oily and to lose flavour.

Madeira. The wine of Madeira varies a great deal in character, rather in the same way as sherry, i.e. from dry and pale to a rich brown. It is drunk chiefly as a dessert wine, and sometimes as an apéritif, depending on the type. A port or sherry glass is used. In cooking Madeira may be added to a brown sauce or *demi-glace* (*sauce madère*) for serving with a beef fillet, braised ham (*jambon à la madère*), and other meat dishes.

Madeira Cake. A classic English cake made of a rich GENOESE mixture with a large proportion of eggs and butter to flour. The characteristic finish is a slice of citron peel baked on top of the cake.

Madeleine. *French:* Small cakes made of a GENOESE mixture and baked traditionally in fluted moulds shaped like a cockle shell.

English: A Victoria sponge mixture baked in round-topped castle-pudding moulds. When cooked the cakes are brushed with a red jam glaze, rolled in desiccated coconut, and topped with a glacé cherry.

Madère. See MADEIRA.

Maid of Honour. A rich almond cheese-cake baked in a puff pastry case. A speciality of Richmond-on-Thames.

Maigre. Without meat, or meatless.

Maître-d'Hôtel. A French term for head waiter or in former times steward of the household. Besides having complete charge of the dining-room or restaurant a *maître d'hôtel* should have a knowledge of cooking. Those dishes which are finished at the table, steak *au poivre*, steak tartare, *crêpes flambées*, etc., are his responsibility.

In cooking, *à la maître-d'hôtel* implies a simple method of preparation or a final touch to finish a dish. The best example of this is *maître-d'hôtel* butter, butter mixed with chopped parsley and sharpened with lemon juice. It is served with grills and fried fish.

Maize. The kernel of INDIAN CORN. Maize meal (Italian *polenta*) is used for puddings, bread, and scones.

Malaga. A very sweet heavy Spanish wine, dark brown in colour. Malaga raisins are large dessert raisins prepared from the muscat grape. They are particularly sweet and good.

Mallard. The largest of the wild ducks and the one most frequently cooked. See DUCK.

Malt. A term given to grain, chiefly barley, in which the starch content has been converted into sugar by incipient fermentation. Used in brewing and distillation. An extract of malt may be added to bread dough for a malt loaf.

Mandarin. See ORANGE.

Mandolin. A vegetable slicer. It consists of a rectangular piece of wood, aluminium, or stainless steel, across which a sharp blade of steel, either plain or fluted, is fixed. The blade can be adjusted by a screw at the side to regulate the thickness of the slice. To slice, the vegetable is rubbed briskly up and down the mandolin.

Mango. Indian fruit usually dark to olive green, but sometimes a rich yellow in colour, and about the size of a goose's egg. The pulp, soft, melting, and juicy like that of a peach, is deep orange with a delicate sweet flavour. There are several varieties, some more highly prized than others. Fresh mangoes, being perishable, were not imported into England until recently. Now, thanks to air transport, mangoes in good condition, though expensive, can be bought here. Tinned mangoes, readily available and more reasonably priced, are excellent either plain or in a fruit salad, or as a fool or water ice.

Maple Syrup. A natural syrup or sap obtained by tapping the sugar maple (*Acer saccharinum*). The syrup is boiled and refined to stop fermentation. Maple syrup is delicious served plain with waffles or hot sweets, or as a flavouring for cold creams or soufflés. It is largely produced in Canada.

Maraschino. A liqueur made chiefly in Zara in Dalmatia. The main ingredient is a type of wild black cherry called *marasca*, from which the name maraschino is derived. The whole cherry is used, the kernels giving the liqueur its particular nutty flavour.

Marc. An abbreviation for *marc eau-de-vie*, a brandy made from the crushed pulp or pressings of wine grapes.

Marengo. A chicken dish named after the battle of Marengo in 1800. The story goes that Napoleon, who did not eat until the battle was decided, seeing the enemy in retreat, ordered his chef Dunand to serve dinner. As Napoleon was well in advance of the baggage wagons a search had to be made for local produce, the result of which was a small chicken, some tomatoes, garlic, oil, three eggs, six fresh-water crayfish, and last but not least a frying-pan. With these Dunand produced a sauté which, liberally sprinkled with brandy from Napoleon's flask and embellished with fried eggs and crayfish, became a famous dish.

Margarine. A fat used largely in cooking, its chief recommendation being that it is cheaper than butter. Margarine may be made of animal fats or vegetable oils. Its best use is in cakes and pastry, which are light and good when made with margarine.

Marinade. A French term for a spiced liquid in which raw meat or fish is soaked or soused before cooking. The purpose of marinading is not only to give flavour but also to help soften the fibres and make the meat tender. Usually a marinade is a mixture of wine, olive oil, sliced onion and carrots, herbs and spices. This is spooned over the meat or fish (*marinade crue*), or brought to the boil and cooled before being used (*marinade cuite*). A marinade may have a small proportion of vinegar in the ingredients, depending on the kind of meat (e.g. venison) to

105

be marinated. The length of time for marinating varies from a few hours to several days.

Marinière. A simple method of cooking shellfish using white wine. It is used particularly for mussels (*moules marinière*). Also a name given to fish dishes garnished with mussels.

Marjoram (*Origanum*). Of the varieties of this herb, sweet marjoram is the one most commonly grown in the herb garden. The flavour is aromatic and goes particularly well in stuffings for veal and lamb.

Marmalade. A conserve or jam made from citrus fruits, especially bitter or Seville oranges which are imported into England in February.

Marmelade. A very well reduced fruit pulp with sugar; more like a fruit cheese than a purée. A popular confection in Spain is made in this way, cut into squares and served as a sweetmeat. A *marmelade* is used principally for a filling, e.g. an apple flan where the filling is baked with the pastry.

Marrons Glacés (French for glazed chestnuts). An expensive confection and one that should be made professionally and not in the domestic kitchen. Large whole chestnuts previously peeled and cooked are poached for many hours in baths of sugar syrup of increasing degrees of density, so that the chestnuts become permeated with the syrup and semi-clear. To glaze them a thicker syrup is beaten lightly until white and the chestnuts dipped in this or coated with it.

Marrow (Bone). A substance, which becomes jelly-like when cooled, found in the centre of the shank-bones of a bullock. Marrow bones make an excellent savoury. They are boiled or steamed, and served, wrapped in small napkins, with hot dry toast. The marrow is scooped out on to the toast with a marrow scoop (an elongated silver or plated spoon), peppered liberally, and eaten piping hot.

Marrow (Vegetable). A late summer vegetable of the gourd family. Marrows are best eaten when they are small, when the flesh is delicate and tender. They should be stewed gently in butter and finished with chopped herbs or parsley, rather than boiled in water. They may also be stuffed and served as a supper dish.

Marsala. A sweet wine made in Sicily, similar in appearance to a Madeira, but inferior in quality. It is used largely in cooking and for sweets such as ZABAGLIONE.

Marzipan. Almond paste. The best marzipan is that made of pounded or ground almonds worked with fondant. Marzipan is used in confectionery and as a coating on wedding or birthday cakes under the top icing.

Matelote. A stew of fish, salt- or fresh-water, cooked with red or white wine according to the region: e.g. *normande*, salt-water fish with white wine and cream; *bourguignonne*, river fish with red wine.

Mayonnaise. A thick rich sauce made from egg-yolks and oil, sharpened with vinegar or lemon juice, served with white meats, fish, or eggs.

Mead. A popular drink in the Middle Ages, mead was brewed from honeycombs after the honey had been extracted and, after fermentation, flavoured with herbs and spices. Nowadays mead is made in England in small quantities, but has lost its popularity.

Measures. In cooking certain standard measures are used for liquids:

1 gill   = $\frac{1}{4}$ pint or 5 fluid ounces
1 pint = 20 fluid ounces
1 quart = 2 pints
4 quarts = 1 gallon

In the north of England a $\frac{1}{2}$ pint is frequently termed a gill.

A standard English measuring cup holds 10 fluid ounces – that is, $\frac{1}{2}$ pint (imperial measure) – whereas an American measuring cup holds 8 fluid ounces, an American $\frac{1}{2}$ pint. When dry ingredients are measured in a cup their weight (avoirdupois) will obviously vary with their density.

AMERICAN MEASURES	ENGLISH EQUIVALENTS
1 cup flour	4 oz.
3 tablespoons flour	1 oz.
1 cup sugar	½ lb.
1 tablespoon sugar	¾ oz.
1 cup butter, margarine, or lard	½ lb.
1 tablespoon butter, margarine, or lard	½ oz.
1 cup uncooked rice	½ lb.

All spoon measurements are level.

METRIC MEASURES	ENGLISH EQUIVALENTS
½ litre	approx. 1 pint
28 grammes	approx. 1 oz.
450 grammes	approx. 1 lb.

Médaillon. Food, usually meat, cut in small rounds or ovals. (See TOURNEDOS.) The term is also used for rounds of *pâte sucrée* iced and marbled with chocolate or icing of a contrasting colour.

Medlar. The fruit of the medlar tree (*Mespilus germanica*). The fruit is about the size of a plum, with a brown skin and firm flesh when gathered. It must, however, be left until the fruit is very ripe and begins to disintegrate before being eaten or used for a preserve such as medlar cheese or jelly.

Melba. The famous dish *pêches Melba* was created by Escoffier for Dame Nellie Melba, the opera singer. It is a ripe peach poached in vanilla syrup, set on vanilla ice cream, and coated with a purée of fresh raspberries (i.e. Melba sauce).

Melon. A fruit of the cucumber family. There are several varieties of melon obtainable in England during the summer. The best known are:

Cantaloup. Medium to large size, recognizable by the natural division into sections on the skin, which is rough. Season, August to September. Expensive to moderate in price.

Charentais. Small and sweet-scented, and green to pale green in colour. Season, late June to August. Expensive to moderate in price.
Honeydew. Large, green, rough-skinned, with pale, honey-flavoured flesh. Season, mid-summer to autumn. Moderate to cheap in price.
Spanish Water. Now frequently called Honeydew. Medium to large with a bright yellow skin. Sweet flesh. Season, late summer to early autumn. Inexpensive.
Water Melons. Very large, with smooth green skin and brilliant red flesh studded with large seeds. Little flavour. Season, summer. Cheap.

Melt. See MILT.

Menu. A programme or list of dishes proposed for a meal. A good, well-planned menu is as important as the meal itself. Nowadays seldom are more than three courses offered for a luncheon; for dinner there may be three to five, according to the occasion. The courses in a dinner menu are as follows: HORS-D'ŒUVRE, soup, fish, ENTRÉE, REMOVE or relevé, SORBET, roast, ENTREMETS, DESSERT; and from these the shortened version may be chosen.

Meringue. Essentially a mixture of egg-whites and sugar, of which there are three varieties:

MERINGUE CHANTILLY (or MERINGUE SUISSE)
Whipped whites with caster sugar folded in. Used for meringues Chantilly, half-shells dried in a slow oven and sandwiched together with crème Chantilly, or to cover the top of a pudding. In the latter, the meringue is dried until the top is crisp but the interior has the consistency of marshmallow.

MERINGUE CUITE
Whites and sugar whisked together until very thick, preferably over gentle heat. Used principally for meringue baskets and petits fours and as a base for creams.

MERINGUE ITALIENNE
Whisked egg-whites on to which a sugar syrup boiled to 260° F. is poured. The whole is then whisked until very thick. Used also for baskets, to cover ice cream for *bombe glacée* or baked alaska, and for *pâtisserie.* Similar to American frosting. See ICING.

Meunière. A method of cooking fish, either small whole fish

109

(e.g. river trout), or fillets (e.g. plaice or sole). The fish is lightly floured and fried in foaming butter until golden-brown. It is then dished, the pan cleaned, and fresh butter added. This is allowed to reach a pale nut-brown when lemon juice and herbs are quickly added. While still foaming this *beurre noisette* is poured over the fish.

Mignonette. Coarse-ground white PEPPER.

Milk. A secretion of the mammary glands. Cows' milk is sold everywhere in England, though goats' milk is also used. Apart from being a highly nutritive drink, milk is much used in cooking and also for cheese-making, and for cream from which butter is obtained. Good milk should contain a fair proportion of fat although this varies according to the breed of cow. Jersey milk is generally considered the richest. The bulk of milk sold in England is pasteurized, i.e. heat-treated as a health precaution (see PASTEURIZE). From the culinary point of view, this is to be deplored, as the process destroys the lactic acid and so precludes the proper souring of the milk. The cream likewise does not rise to the surface of the milk so readily, and so it is not worth while to leave the milk to stand for the cream to set.

Mille-Feuille (literally 'a thousand leaves'). A name given to a *pâtisserie* made of layers of puff pastry baked until crisp, and layered alternately with whipped cream and raspberry or strawberry jam, or with pastry cream. The top is iced with a thin white fondant or glacé icing. The *mille-feuille* is cut into slices for serving. In England these are sometimes called vanilla slices. A *gâteau mille-feuille* consists of large rings of baked puff pastry built up one on top of the other, the centre being filled with fruit and cream.

Milt (or Melt). The soft roe of a fish, e.g. soft roes from the male herring. In meat, the melt is the spleen of an animal, so called as at one time it was believed to carry out the same function as the soft roe.

Mincemeat. The filling of a mince-pie, the word coming from the French *émincer*, to chop up finely. Traditionally mincemeat contained meat as well as apples, suet, and fruit. Nowadays the meat is omitted. Good mincemeat should be laced with brandy or rum before being stored in jars for use.

Minestra and **Minestrone.** These broth soups are very alike; minestra is reputed to be Spanish in origin, and minestrone, Italian. Minestra is now generally accepted as being a purely vegetable soup while minestrone contains bacon and ham as well as fresh and dried vegetables. Grated Parmesan cheese always accompanies these soups.

Mint. One of the best-known kitchen herbs. As well as the ordinary garden herb there are several varieties worth growing.

BOWLES VARIETY (*Mentha rotundifolia*)
This is the best to grow in place of the ordinary mint. It is ideal for mint sauce and general kitchen use as it does not revert to wild mint with its rather hard spearmint flavour. A handsome plant, growing 2–3 feet high, with a soft green furry leaf, sweet and aromatic.

APPLE MINT
Variegated leaf and strong smell, good in fruit drinks and chutneys.

EAU-DE-COLOGNE MINT
Red-brown leaf, and a strong scent of eau-de-cologne.

PINEAPPLE MINT
Dark green leaf and a strong smell of pineapple. Delicious infused in fruit cups, tomato juice, vinegars, etc.

Mirepoix. A mixture of root vegetables cut into small squares or dice, with or without the addition of a small quantity of raw ham or bacon. Used principally as a base for braising meat and for certain sauces to give flavour.

Mocha. A variety of coffee bean grown in Mocha in Arabia. In cooking, 'mocha' implies anything flavoured with coffee.

Molasses. See TREACLE.

Monosodium Glutamate. Glutamic acid occurs in many proteins. Hydrolysis of these proteins gives the free acid which on neutralization yields monosodium glutamate. It is used as a flavour enhancer although it is usually stated to have no flavour of its own. The types of canned product in which it is used are meat and fish, stews and soups. It is also used in sausages, bouillon cubes, beef extract and similar savoury products. When monosodium glutamate is used in tomato purée it depresses the metallic and bitter taste.

Morel. An edible fungus. There are several varieties of morel, the commonest being *Morchella esculenta*, found in wood clearings and hedgerows in spring. They are easily distinguished as they have a sponge-like or honeycombed cap. The colour is yellowish-brown to grey. Morels may be stewed or fried, or dried and used for flavouring.

Morello. A dark red semi-translucent CHERRY, in season in late July, early August. It is tart and acid in flavour and is therefore much prized for jam-making and for cherry brandy.

Mornay. A term applied to a dish, usually fish, egg, or vegetable, that is coated with a Mornay sauce (a *béchamel* to which cheese is added). Once coated the dish is usually glazed, i.e. browned under the grill.

Mortadella. See CONTINENTAL SAUSAGES.

Morue (French for salt dried cod). The classic ingredient of a *brandade*. Like most dried foods the fish should be well soaked before use.

Moselle. A fine white wine, somewhat like Hock, from the valley of the Mosel in Germany. Moselle comes in the same tall elegant bottles as Hock but the glass is green instead of brown.

Mould. A container used to shape a certain mixture or ingredient. There are a variety of moulds, the best known of which are:

Bombe. The traditional mould for the shaping of ice cream, e.g. *bombe glacée.* When filled with cream or water ice bombe moulds were buried in a mixture of ice and salt, and so were usually made of copper with a tight-fitting lid.

112

Border. A plain mould in the shape of a ring with a flat top, so that fillets of fish, cutlets, etc. could be arranged on the top of a vegetable cream or jelly cooked or set in the mould.

Charlotte. A plain mould similar to a cake-tin in appearance but with slightly sloping sides designed to take the fingers of sponge or bread which line the mould, the chief characteristic of a CHARLOTTE.

Cornet. An individual mould, conical in shape, and made of metal or paper. Metal cornets are used to make pastry cases to hold a sweet or savoury mixture, e.g. cream horns. Puff pastry is wrapped round the outside and baked. They are also used to shape slices of ham, etc., which are to be filled with a mousse. Paper cornets are used for piping small quantities of icing, cream, etc., for decoration, or to fill *petits choux* or *éclairs*.

Dariole or *Castle Pudding Mould*. An individual plain cylindrical mould used for steaming or baking mixtures and for setting sweet or savoury creams, e.g. prawns in aspic.

Savarin. A plain ring mould similar to a border mould but with a rounded top. Designed for SAVARINS.

Timbale. A plain straight-sided mould, which may be the shape of a high border or charlotte mould. Sometimes made with a tube in the middle, and called a tube mould. Timbales are used for meat or fish creams. To serve something *en timbale* also means to pile it up in a circular arrangement in the dish.

Moussáka. A savoury dish (of Turkish origin) of spiced mutton, tomato, and aubergine topped with a cheese sauce.

Mousse. A smooth, light, rich cream, either sweet or savoury. The chief ingredients of a sweet mousse are eggs, egg-yolks, and cream. The mousse may be frozen or set with gelatine. For a savoury mousse, fish or meat enriched with cream are used.

Mousseline. As MOUSSE but also the name for a sauce of eggs and cream.

Muesli. A Swiss dish made for breakfast or as a pudding. Muesli is a mixture of uncooked rolled oats, raw diced apple or other fruit and cream. Served cold.

Muffin. An English teacake. Muffins are rarely seen nowadays, apart from home-made ones. The batter is similar to that of

CRUMPETS (i.e. made with yeast), but muffins are slightly thicker and browned on both sides. Metal rings (muffin rings) can be bought and these are set on a baking-sheet. The mixture is poured in and the muffins baked. When set and risen, the muffin and ring are turned over to brown the other side. Muffins are pulled apart, not cut, for buttering and serving hot. At one time a muffin man carrying muffins and crumpets on a tray balanced on his head came round the London streets on Sunday afternoons throughout the winter, ringing a hand-bell to advertise his wares.

Mulberry. The fruit of the mulberry tree (*Morus nigra*). Mulberries are not grown or sold commercially in England. The leaves of the mulberry are food for silkworms, while the fruit resembles a large blackberry and is sweetly acid in flavour. Mulberries are good as a compote or syrup.

Mullet. There are two varieties of mullet, red and grey. The former is a small fish with a rosy pink skin and friable white flesh, easily distinguished by a short barb underneath its chin. The liver is much prized and is frequently left in the fish after it has been cleaned through the gills, thus earning its name as the woodcock of the sea. The season is May to September. The grey mullet is a much larger fish running from 3 to 6 lb., silvery in colour and resembling a bass. The flesh is firm and white. Grey mullet are caught in shoals off the Cornish coast in the early summer months continuing into the autumn. They can be cooked in the same way as haddock or cod.

Mulligatawny. A peppery, curry-flavoured soup, either thick or clear, much in vogue early in the twentieth century.

Mushroom (*Agaricus campester* or *Psalliota campestris*, the common or field mushroom). Though these are found in fields in late summer or early autumn they are also extensively cultivated. In fact, owing to the lack of horse manure, wild mushrooms are less common than formerly, and the cultivated ones are widely sold and comparatively inexpensive. Cultivated mushrooms are divided into three main grades: buttons, caps, and flats. The last are generally considered to have the best flavour, though they do not keep so well. *Champignons de Paris* are small, firm, white button mushrooms.

Mussel. Small salt-water shellfish, blue-black in colour, at one time called the oyster of the poor owing to its cheapness. Mussels are usually eaten cooked, either as a kind of stew (*moules marinière*) or cold, soused in vinegar. They also form a garnish with other shellfish. Mussels are best from September to April, and are sold by the measure, e.g. a quart, rather than by weight.

Mustard. The seed of the plant *Sinapis alba*, a species of *Brassica*. The word mustard is derived from 'must' or vinegar in which the seeds were boiled. English mustard is sold as a fine flour which is mixed with vinegar or water before use. French mustards, sold in the form of paste, often have herbs added to the powdered mustard seed. Mustard seed is used as a spice for pickles.

Mustard (Salad). The first sprouting from the seeds of mustard. This type of mustard is grown and sold in small punnets. It can also be grown at home on light soil, in seed boxes or on damp flannel in a warm room. See also CRESS.

Mutton. Flesh of a sheep over 8 months old. Good mutton, especially that of the black-faced sheep, is excellent and may be roasted, braised, or stewed. See LAMB for a diagram of cuts.

Nasturtium (*Tropaeolum*). A decorative garden plant which may also be used in the kitchen. When pickled the seeds make a good substitute for capers. A few flowers and young leaves add colour and a spicy flavour to a salad. The seeds are hot and peppery; the leaves and flowers are similar to watercress in taste.

Navarin. A French word for a brown lamb or mutton stew with root vegetables. See HARICOT.

Neapolitan Ice. Any simple fruit or cream ice made in a plain 'brick' mould. Though they can be of one colour there are usually several different-coloured layers.

Nectarine. A delicious late summer fruit grown under glass in England. A nectarine is a variety of peach but with a smooth skin and somewhat smaller. Like a peach the skin is flushed with red and the flesh fragrant and melting.

Needles. Kitchen equipment essential to advanced cookery.

(1) TRUSSING NEEDLES
Steel needles of varying lengths from 5 to 8 in. with a large eye to carry the string. Used for trussing and sewing up joints and birds after stuffing.

(2) LARDING NEEDLE
Made in the same lengths as trussing needles but tapering in thickness. At the eye end the needle is split down $\frac{1}{2}$–1 in. into 4 or 5 flanges. These hold the LARDON securely while the needle is drawn through the meat. See LARDING.

Nesselrode. The name given to a once fashionable iced pudding,

invented by Mouy, the chef of a famous Russian, Count Nesselrode. The base is ice cream, flavoured with maraschino and
mixed with a chestnut purée and dried fruits. The whole was
frozen in a tall plain mould, and before being turned out for
serving, decorated with *marrons glacés*.

Nettle. A common weed which can be pleasant as a vegetable,
cooked like spinach, if gathered when the shoots are young and
tender, in March or early April. A home-made 'beer' can be
made from nettles.

Niçois. The name given to dishes from the district around Nice.
They are composed of foods – fish, vegetables, etc. – that are
common to the region. Food cooked *à la niçoise* has as a main
ingredient or garnish tomatoes, garlic, black olives, anchovies,
and olive oil.

Noisette. Flavoured with or made of hazelnuts. A term also
used to describe a 'nut' of meat, e.g. 'noisettes of lamb', meat
rolled and cut without the bone. See also BEURRE NOISETTE.

Nonpareil. Tiny sugar sweets known as 'hundreds and thousands'. Also small CAPERS are graded as 'nonpareils'.

Noodle. Long ribbon-like PASTA, cooked in the same way as
spaghetti, etc. The paste can be used for other shapes (see
RAVIOLI) and is made with flour and water, sometimes with
the addition of eggs.

Normandy Pippin. Normandy Pippins are whole apples, peeled,
cored, and dried. They are rarely seen nowadays, but are delicious if well soaked before being gently stewed in syrup flavoured
with lemon until very tender.

Nougat. There are two varieties of nougat. (1) *White nougat*, for
which Montélimart is famous. This is a confection of boiled
sugar and white of egg mixed with choice nuts and dried cherries. The whole is set in shallow tins between sheets of rice
paper before being cut into small rectangles. (2) *Caramel or
almond nougat*. Caster sugar melted to a caramel with chopped
browned almonds stirred into it. When turned on to an oiled

marble, the nougat can be moulded to make baskets, etc. or cut into shapes for decorating sweets and cakes.

Noyau. A liqueur made of brandy, flavoured with fruit kernels.

Nut. A general term for the fruit of certain trees that have a hard shell in which the kernel, or nut, lies. See ALMOND, CHESTNUT, COCONUT, FILBERT, HAZELNUT, and WALNUT.

Nutmeg. The fruit or seeds of the nutmeg tree after the MACE is taken off. Nutmeg is a pungent spice and should be used sparingly to flavour sauces and sweets. It should be grated on an especially fine grater.

Oatcake. One of the oldest forms of unleavened bread. Indigenous to the north of England, Wales, and Scotland. The cakes are made from oatmeal, water, and a small quantity of fat to make the paste 'bind'. The method of making varies according to the district, oatcakes in the West Riding being made more from a batter than a paste. This used to be thrown on to a heated iron plate and when firm enough was peeled off and hung up to dry. In Wales and Scotland the paste is rolled out thinly and cut into rounds or triangles (farls) before being cooked on a girdle or in a cool oven.

Oatmeal. Ground from oats. It is said that the more northerly grown oats have the finest flavour, Midlothian oatmeal being considered the best. Oatmeal can be bought in three grades, coarse, medium, and fine, coarse and medium being the most used for porridge, black and white puddings, and haggis, and fine for oatcakes and scones.

Octopus, Cuttlefish, Ink Fish, Squid. All these belong to the same family and inhabit the Mediterranean and Atlantic waters. The body and tentacles of the smaller octopus are eaten cut into strips and made into a stew. Long slow cooking is essential as octopus can be very tough. The tentacles can be cut across into rings, first cooked until tender, then dipped into batter and fried. Fresh squid is sold in England and may be cooked in the same way or stewed with wine and onions.

Offal. A term given to the 'insides' of an animal slaughtered for food. Heart, liver, lights, kidneys, melt, ox tail, sweetbreads, tongues come under this heading.

Oil. A clear fluid extracted from various vegetable and animal substances. The best known are olive, almond, groundnut, maize, cod-liver, and whale oil. Oil has many uses in the kitchen, in salad dressings, sauces, for frying and so on. Olive oil is considered the best, particularly for salad dressings, as it has the finest flavour; but it is the most expensive. Useful all-purpose oils are those which are deodorized, such as groundnut. This is sold under various proprietary names and is inexpensive.

Okra (*Hibiscus esculentus*). Sometimes called 'Ladies' fingers'. The young green pods resemble small gherkins and are used for making a soup or stew called gumbo. Okra is a native of the West Indies, but is now grown in India and America. It can be bought in tins and makes a good vegetable mixed with a sharp tomato sauce or in a curry.

Olive. The fruit of the olive tree (*Olea europoea*) largely cultivated in the south of France, Spain, Greece, and Italy. Those from Spain are considered to be the finest in both size and flavour. Green olives, the unripe fruit, are preserved in brine and eaten as an apéritif or savoury. They may also be included in salads and sauces to add piquancy. Green olives are also sold stoned and stuffed with pimento or anchovies. Black olives, the ripe fruit, sweet and aromatic in flavour, are also eaten as a savoury or in salads. OIL is extracted from the ripe fruit.

Omelet. An egg dish. There are two main varieties: the plain or French omelet and the soufflé or fluffy omelet. The former is usually savoury, made with the whole eggs beaten together; for the latter the eggs are separated, the whites being whipped before being incorporated with the yolks. Omelets are cooked in a thick iron or aluminium frying-pan with curved sides, known as an omelet pan. The essentials for a good omelet are a thick, not too large pan, fresh butter and eggs, quick heat, and fast cooking. The omelets may be stuffed with various mixtures before being turned out and served. For a Spanish omelet the whole beaten eggs are mixed with diced cooked vegetables, cooked in the pan like a pancake and served flat.

Onion (*Allium*). A fleshy root, and one of the most valued flavourings in the kitchen. Onions are available all the year round but are at their best from early autumn, when the crop is gathered, to late spring. The main types of onion are:

(1) THE ALL-PURPOSE ONION
Medium to large size. There are several varieties ranging from the dark-brown to the pale-golden skinned.

(2) SPANISH ONION
Very large and mild flavoured, ideal for boiling or braising.

(3) BUTTON or PICKLING ONION
Small and brown-skinned, with white flesh; used principally for garnishes or for pickling.

(4) SILVER-SKIN ONION
Smaller than the pickling onion, with a silver skin and pure white flesh; used for pickling.

(5) GREEN ONIONS
Under this heading come (*a*) spring onions, usually the thinnings of the ordinary onion; and (*b*) Welsh onions or stone leeks, like spring onions but growing in clusters. Syboes is a Scots word for spring or Welsh onions. Scallion has much the same meaning but can also mean SHALLOT.

Orange. A well-known citrus fruit, the juice of which is rich in vitamin C, and the zest and pith in pectin. There are two main kinds: the sweet, of which there are several varieties; and the bitter, the Seville or Bigarade orange. The bitter orange is imported into England chiefly for MARMALADE and for flavouring. See BIGARADE. Oranges are available all the year round, but are at their best and most plentiful from autumn to late spring. They are imported principally from Spain, Israel (Jaffa), and South Africa. Mandarins also belong to this family, and so do clementines and tangerines. These last three appear for a comparatively short season during the winter months. See also SATSUMA.

121

Orange-flower Water. A distilled infusion of orange flowers used for flavouring, principally sponge cakes. Obtainable at good chemists'.

Oregano (*Origanum vulgaris*). Common or wild MARJORAM.

Orly. Strip or whole fillet of white fish, e.g. haddock or whiting, dipped into fritter batter and fried. Served with a tomato sauce.

Osso Bucho. An Italian dish. Round slices of veal taken from the knuckle with the bone left in the centre are usually braised with a rich brown or tomato sauce.

Ox Tail. Classed as offal. Ox tail makes a delicious rich stew and is also famous as soup.

Ox Tongue. Also classed as offal. Ox tongues weigh from 3 to 6 lb. Usually sold salted for boiling or braising. When served cold the tongue is pressed after skinning.

Oyster. Shellfish, in season from September to April. There are various kinds of oyster: the best-known and most obtainable in England are the Whitstable 'natives'. These are also cultivated along the Essex coast and in Cornwall. In France the *huîtres de Belon* are well known, as are the green oysters or *huîtres de Marennes*. Eaten with a little lemon juice and cayenne pepper oysters are highly nutritive. If served hot the minimum amount of cooking time is necessary. They may be grilled in the shell with a dusting of Parmesan cheese, wrapped in bacon for a savoury (ANGELS ON HORSEBACK), or put in a soufflé.

Paëlla. A colourful Spanish dish of rice, shellfish, chicken, and vegetables cooked together, and well spiced with garlic. It is frequently served in the dish in which it is cooked, a shallow earthenware or metal pan.

Palestine. A name given to a soup made from the Jerusalem ARTICHOKE.

Panada. A basic thickening for meat, fish, and vegetable creams, and forcemeats. A panada may be: crumbs soaked in milk or stock; a paste of water, butter, and flour made in the same way as chou pastry; or a thick *béchamel* sauce.

Pancake. A thin batter of eggs and flour cooked or fried in a thick frying-pan to form wafer-thin cakes. These may be served with lemon quarters and dusted with caster sugar, or stuffed with a savoury filling. Pancakes are traditionally served on Shrove Tuesday.

Papaya. A tropical South American fruit which is sweet and easily digestible. The juice has the property of making meat tender. See TENDERIZE.

Papillote. A paper case. Cooking *en papillote* means placing the raw food, e.g. small whole fish such as herring or red mullet, or cutlets, on rounds of buttered greaseproof paper with seasonings. One side of the paper is then folded over the food, and the two edges are pleated and folded together. Papillotes are baked for 15–20 minutes in a moderate oven. The paper is removed before serving. This method of cooking preserves the juices of the food.

Paprika. A pepper made from pimentoes or sweet red peppers. There are various types, used for different dishes. Paprika is spicy rather than hot. Hungarian in origin. See CAPSICUM.

Parboil. To boil until half-cooked, e.g. potatoes before they are roasted.

Parkin. A Yorkshire spiced gingerbread made with a high proportion of oatmeal. It is baked in a shallow tin such as a roasting-tin and cut into squares when cold. Parkin is best kept for several days before being eaten.

Parma (Ham). A smoked ham from Parma. The ham is cut in wafer-thin slices and served raw as a first course. It is the ham used to serve with ripe melon (*prosciutto mellone*) or figs.

Parmentier. The name given to a dish which contains or has a garnish of potato, e.g. *potage Parmentier*, cream of potato soup. The name comes from Antoine-Auguste Parmentier, a French agronomist living in the eighteenth century who did much to popularize the potato.

Parmesan. A large, exceptionally hard cheese from the district of Parma. Made from skimmed milk, Parmesan has a rich and spicy flavour and is ideal as a cooking cheese. It is the only cheese that does not become elastic when heated, and is the classic accompaniment to pasta dishes and some soups, e.g. minestrone. Mixed with Gruyère it makes a perfect Mornay sauce for a gratin. Parmesan should be bought in the piece and grated as required.

Parsley (*Carum*). A biennial, known as the herb of health. Largely used in the kitchen, the stalks in a *bouquet garni*, the fronds chopped and used as a flavouring or garnish. Whole sprays are also fried to serve with fried fish, etc.

Parsnip. A winter root vegetable, with a creamy white flesh, and tapering root. After being peeled it may be sliced in rounds or cut into fingers before being cooked. Parsnips may be boiled and then mashed with butter, fried in butter or dripping. The flavour is sweet and somewhat aromatic.

Partridge. A small game bird in season from 1 September to 1 February. There are two varieties, the grey or European partridge being the most common in the British Isles. The French or red-legged partridge is a slightly larger bird and is occasionally found in England, especially in East Anglia. The grey partridge is the most prized in the kitchen for its fine flavour, the young birds being best served plainly roasted with the usual accompaniments for game, i.e. game chips, fried crumbs, and a clear strong gravy. Older birds are excellent casseroled, or boned, stuffed, and braised.

Pashka (Russian). A rich sweet made of curd cheese and cream, containing chopped almonds and dried fruit; it is set in a special wooden mould. A speciality made for Easter.

Passion Fruit. The fruit of the passion flower vine or granadilla, a native of South America. Sometimes imported fresh into England.

Pasta. Italian for a farinaceous paste of flour and water, cut into various shapes, e.g. spaghetti, tagliatelle, macaroni, etc. Pasta is bought dried, but if made at home it can be cooked as soon as it is made.

Pasteurize. Pasteur's method of heating milk to sterilize it and to prevent fermentation. The milk is heated to a temperature between 130 and 160° F. and maintained there for some time before cooling. See MILK.

Pastry. A mixture of fat and flour bound with water, which can be sweet or savoury, boiled or baked.

There are several types using varying proportions and kinds of fat.

ENGLISH PASTRIES
Short-crust: for fruit pies and flans.
Flaky: for sausage rolls and meat pies.
Rough-puff: as flaky, and also for jam puffs and apple dumplings.
Puff-paste: for bouchées, *vol-au-vents*, *mille-feuilles*, etc.
Suet-crust: for roly-polys, steak and kidney pudding.
Hot-water-crust: for raised pies of all kinds.

Pastry Cream

FRENCH AND CONTINENTAL PASTES
  Pâte brisée: for pies and savoury flans.
  Pâte sucrée: for flans, tartlets, and *pâtisseries*.
  Pâte frolle (almond): for flans and *gâteaux*.

Pastry Cream (French, *crème pâtissière*). Sometimes called pastry custard. A cream made with egg-yolks, flour, cornflour, sugar, and milk. Once boiled the cream is lightened with whipped egg-whites. When cold it is the traditional filling for éclairs, flavoured with coffee or chocolate, etc. Flavoured with vanilla, orange, etc., it is used to fill flans, tartlets and other *pâtisserie*.

Pasty. See PATTY.

Pâte. See PASTRY.

Pâté. French for pie. The term should apply only to meat or fish dishes enclosed in pastry, but it is also used for a meat mixture cooked in a terrine without a crust, e.g. *pâté de veau*, *pâté de campagne*.

Pâtisserie. A French term for small cakes or pastries.

Patty. A small or individual pie, made with short-crust, flaky, or puff pastry. The word can also apply to a *bouchée* and is a corruption of pasty. A patty pan is a tartlet mould. See TURNOVER.

Paupiette (French). Thin slices of beef or veal spread with a savoury forcemeat, rolled up to form a sausage, tied, and braised (e.g. beef olives). *Paupiettes* of sole (fillets of sole spread with a fish farce and rolled up) are poached and coated with a sauce.

Paysanne. Cooked in peasant fashion, i.e. braised meat or poultry accompanied by a garnish of carrots, turnips, celery, onions, etc.

Pea. A familiar vegetable of which there are several varieties, maturing early or late. A good pea has a juicy pod well filled with small to medium-sized peas which should never be allowed

126

to grow too large. The pod when pressed should give with a gentle pop. The round or marrowfat pea is considered the best for canning. Another variety is the French *mange-tout*, which has a particularly fleshy pod with a few small peas inside. As the name implies the whole pod is eaten. Green peas are the classic accompaniment to roast duck and spring lamb, plainly boiled with a sprig of mint and finished with a knob of butter. See also CHICK-PEA and SPLIT PEA.

Peach. A fruit, grown in England on a sunny wall or under glass and largely imported from the Mediterranean countries and South Africa. There are two main varieties, the white-fleshed or English peach with soft melting flesh and a particularly fine flavour, and the Hale peach with a firm yet juicy flesh, deep yellow in colour. The Hale peach, which is larger than the English variety, is the one most frequently used for canning and preserving. Both have a soft, plush-like skin flushed with deep pink to red. Peaches are most plentiful from late July to mid-September. South African peaches arrive in England around Christmas.

Peanut. (Also known as monkey nuts and groundnuts.) Small kernels with a pinky brown skin carried in a rough pale-brown pod-shaped husk, two kernels to a nut. They have a pronounced flavour and may be eaten raw or roasted and salted. Peanuts are used for making *peanut butter*, which can be eaten in sandwiches or on toast, and peanut OIL, marketed as groundnut oil.

Pear. There are numerous varieties of pears; some are grown for dessert, others for cooking. The latter are of small to medium size and very hard. Peeled and simmered in the oven whole or halved, in a thin syrup with a strip of lemon rind, until they turn rich red brown, they are delicious. Of English dessert pears there are several varieties, which mature at different times throughout the early autumn and winter. Pears also reach England in summer from Italy and in early spring from South Africa. Pears must be eaten in the pink of condition and this is not easy to determine. They can quickly become over-ripe or 'sleepy'.

Pearl Barley

BEST-KNOWN DESSERT VARIETIES

William's Bon Chretien or *Williams Pear*. Very smooth skin flushed with pink. White sweet flesh, exceptionally juicy. Medium size. An early pear, maturing in late August and September.

Conference. A brown green skin, elongated in shape. Creamy-yellow flesh of a fine flavour. A later pear maturing in October.

Doyenne de Comice. A very large, fine pear with a roughish brown skin and creamy-white flesh. Flavour exceptionally good. At its best late November and December.

Beurre Hardy. A firm-fleshed rather round pear with a dark green smooth skin. Flesh white and juicy, and it has a good flavour. Largely imported into England.

Pearl Barley. See BARLEY.

Pease Pudding. Classic accompaniment to a piece of boiled pork. SPLIT PEAS are well soaked and then boiled in a cloth for an hour or two. They are then turned out and well mashed with butter, pepper and salt. After this the pudding is put back into the cloth and boiled with the pork for a further half-hour or so. An egg may be added with the butter if wished.

Pecan. The nut of a species of hickory tree indigenous to the southern and western states of North America. When shelled, the nuts resemble walnut kernels.

Pectin. A substance found in the pith of citrus fruit, from which it can be extracted. Some fruits, such as red- and black-currants, are rich in pectin; others, such as strawberries, have very little. Pectin is necessary to make jams and jellies set or 'jell'. Commercially prepared pectin may be bought for making jams of fruits low in pectin content.

Pepper. The fruit or berry (peppercorn) of the pepper plant. Peppercorns can be either black or white: the black being the whole berry picked before it is ripe; and the white the ripe fruit freed from pulp and skin. White peppercorns after they are coarsely ground are known as mignonnette pepper. Ground pepper is produced from either black or white peppercorns, the black having the more pungent and aromatic flavour. Ground

128

pepper quickly loses its flavour so it is advisable to grind it as required. See ALLSPICE and CAPSICUM.

Peppermint. One of the mint family. Found wild, and cultivated for its oil.

Perch. A fresh-water fish found in lakes and rivers. The flesh is white and friable but full of bones. Little culinary value.

Périgord. A town and district in France famed for truffles and good, rich cooking. A dish cooked *à la périgourdine* includes truffles and sometimes *foie gras*.

Perry. A drink made from pears, as CIDER is made from apples.

Persimmon. A round smooth-skinned fruit which resembles a tomato in appearance. As it ripens the skin turns from yellow to red. The flesh is tart in flavour. Persimmons may be eaten raw or used for drinks.

Pestle and Mortar. A piece of kitchen equipment used for pounding certain ingredients to make them smooth (e.g. for fish or meat creams). The mortar is a thick bowl of marble, stone or metal, and the pestle (which should be of wood) is used for pounding. The work of the mortar has largely been taken over by the electric blender or emulsifier.

Petite Marmite. A consommé strongly flavoured with chicken, which takes its name from the *marmite* or earthenware soup pot.

Petits Fours. A name used for many kinds of small fancy cakes and biscuits.

Pheasant. A game bird in season from 1 October to 1 February. Pheasants are particularly handsome birds, usually sold by the brace. The hen bird though smaller is considered to have the finer flavour, and to be more succulent. Pheasants should be hung 5–7 days, according to the weather, before cooking. The flesh is slightly gamey and inclined to be dry, so care must be taken in cooking. Pheasants may be roasted or casseroled or pot-roasted.

Physalis. Botanical name for CAPE GOOSEBERRY.

Piccalilli. A pickle of mixed vegetables in a mustard sauce.

Pickle. A strong solution of brine used for salting beef, tongue, etc.

Pickles. Onions, cucumber, cauliflower, and other vegetables preserved in spiced vinegar.

Pie. Meat, game, or fruit cooked in a dish (pie-dish) and covered with a pastry crust. Meat or game completely enclosed in a pie crust is known as a raised pie, e.g. pork pie. Special moulds are sold for making these.

Pig. The pig is perhaps our most valued meat-giving animal. It supplies fresh meat as pork, and also bacon, gammon, and hams both smoked and unsmoked. It has been said about the pig that the only inedible thing is the squeal, everything else being turned to some account. Pigs are specially bred for the table (porkers) and for bacon (baconers), and the method of cutting them up differs accordingly. See also PORK and SUCKING PIG.

Pigeon. A small bird classed as game, but in season throughout the year. The wild or wood pigeon is the most common, but the best are birds specially bred for the table. See SQUAB.

Pike. A large fresh-water fish with white friable flesh, especially suitable for the making of QUENELLES. Pike may also be stuffed and roasted whole.

Pikelet. Yorkshire for DROP SCONE, girdle cake, or Scotch pancake. Also a name given to crumpets.

Pilau (or Pilaff). Rice cooked in stock until the grains are tender and the liquid absorbed. Chicken or other meat and herbs and spices may be cooked with the rice.

Pilchard. Small fish caught off the Cornish coast, similar to a herring but smaller. Used mostly for canning.

Pimento. Sweet pepper. The name commonly given to the tinned red pepper, while the fresh, whether red or green, are called (sweet) peppers. See ALLSPICE and CAPSICUM.

Pineapple. A delicious tropical fruit, best eaten raw. Pineapples are obtainable all the year round but vary very much in price according to the season. They may be used for various sweet dishes – ices, sherbets, jams, cakes – and for drinks. If it is to be used in a jelly or cream with gelatine the pineapple must first be cooked.

Pine Nut or **Kernel.** Edible nuts of some pine trees. They resemble almonds in flavour.

Pirozhki (Russian cookery). Small savoury turnovers. The pastry is made with yeast, similar to a brioche dough, with a filling of meat, fish, cheese, or vegetables. The pirozhki are then fried or baked. They may also take the form of pancakes rolled up round the filling. Pirozhki are eaten with soup (e.g. borsch) or as part of *zakouska*, Russian *hors-d'œuvre*.

Pissaladière. A tart or flan from the district of Nice, filled with onions and tomatoes, and garnished with anchovy fillets and black olives.

Pistachio. The nut of the pistacia tree (*Pistacia vera*). The nuts are small with a bright green kernel and a sweet, slightly aromatic flavour. They are dried like almonds and are much used in confectionery, e.g. white nougat, and to flavour creams and ices. They may also be salted like almonds.

Pith. The white part of a citrus fruit lying between the zest or coloured rind and the flesh. The pith contains PECTIN.

Pithivier. A round flat *gâteau* made of puff pastry with a filling of rich almond paste. A speciality of the town of Pithivier in France.

Pizza (Italian cookery). There are several kinds of pizza, that from Naples being the most famous. A pizza is a flat round of light bread dough, covered with tomatoes, anchovy fillets, and slices of soft cheese (mozzarella or Bel Paese). The pizza is brushed with olive oil before being baked. It should be eaten fresh from the oven.

Plaice. A medium-sized flat fish, creamy white with a reddish tinge on one side, and a grey brown with orange or red spots on the other. Plaice are common in European waters, and though the flesh is rather tasteless it is well thought of in England. Filleted, it is best fried.

Plantain. Very like a banana, for which it is often mistaken. Plantains are larger than the true banana with a firmer and slightly more fibrous flesh. For this reason they are good for frying, for fritters, or for baking.

Pluck. The heart, entrails, and lights of an animal. According to some sources so called because they are plucked out after slaughtering.

Plum (*Prunus domesticus*). A late summer to early autumn fruit of which there are many varieties, both dessert and cooking.

BEST-KNOWN VARIETIES

Victoria. A large oval plum, red and yellow in colour, and excellent in flavour. Good for dessert, cooking, jam, and bottling. August.

Early Rivers. Small red plum, sweet, and excellent for cooking, jam, spicing, and bottling. Late July, early August.

Yellow or Gage. Large, yellowish green, best for cooking and jam-making. Also a small 'greengage' plum suitable for dessert but not so fine as a true greengage.

Czar. Large purple plum, best eaten raw, fair flavour. Late.

Damson. See DAMSON.

Mirabelle. Small round yellowish sweet-scented plum not often seen in England. Similar to the cherry plum, a small, bright red cooking plum. End of July, early August.

Poaching. A method of gentle cooking in water or other liquid. The temperature should not exceed 190–200° F., i.e. when the liquid barely trembles and, in the case of water, small crystal bubbles appear on the bottom and sides of the pan. Eggs, fish, fruit (i.e. poached in syrup) may be cooked by this method.

Poivrade. A piquant sauce based on a *demi-glace*. Reduced white wine or vinegar is added with chopped gherkin and herbs. Used for meats such as steak, cutlets, liver, and brains.

Polenta. Italian for maize (corn) meal, used in making *gnocchi* and in bread and cakes. A good substitute is semolina.

Polonaise, à la. A garnish used chiefly for cauliflower and asparagus. Fry fresh white breadcrumbs in butter until crisp and golden-brown and pour both butter and crumbs over the cooked vegetables. Sprinkle the dish with sieved hard-boiled egg-yolks mixed with chopped parsley. The white may also be chopped or shredded and used to garnish the dish.

Pomegranate (*Punica granatum*). The fruit of the pomegranate tree, which grows largely in North Africa. As the name implies, a pomegranate is like an apple with grains, and has a rough, reddish-brown skin, filled with large seeds embedded in a red pulp. The flavour is tart and delicious; the juice is used to make the syrup known as *grenadine* and for flavouring ices and jellies.

Pontac. A ketchup made of elderberry juice and boned anchovies.

Poppy Seed. The fine grey seeds of the opium poppy (*Papaver somniferum*) are used for sprinkling over rolls and breads before baking.

Pork. The flesh of a PIG. The best pork is that known as 'dairy fed', where the pigs are fed on milk and specially fattened. Smaller and leaner pork is now being bred for the table. Pork is also salted or pickled and is then boiled before being served hot or cold. Roast pork with apple sauce is a classic dish, as is boiled pork, salt or fresh, with pease pudding. See BACON and HAM.

Porridge. A mixture of oatmeal and salted water cooked together to a thick cream. Medium or coarse oatmeal is best, and either may be used according to taste. Well salted water is brought to the boil and the oatmeal sprinkled in, approximately one handful to one pint of water. The mixture is then well stirred with a porridge stick (spurtle) or wooden spoon, and put to cook gently for $\frac{3}{4}$ hour or so. It should be stirred from time to time. Porridge is frequently made in a double saucepan to avoid burning. Porridge is now largely a breakfast dish but at one time was the staple diet in Scotland. It should be eaten piping hot with cold milk, the spoon being first dipped into the hot porridge and then into the milk. To most Scots, porridge needs no other accompaniment, except a little additional salt, but many people like to eat it with sugar and cream.

Port. Port is a fortified wine produced in Portugal. It is essentially a dessert wine but is also used in the preparation of certain dishes, e.g. jugged hare.

Porterhouse Steak (American T-bone steak). A slice or steak of about 1½ in. thick cut from the wing-rib of beef.

Portugaise, à la. Containing tomato or strongly flavoured with tomato.

Posset. A hot drink made from milk to which is added wine, ale, or treacle, whose acidity curdles the milk. It is usually strained before it is served. It used to be a household remedy for coughs and colds.

Potato (*Solanum tuberosum*). A staple food, high in calories.

Pork

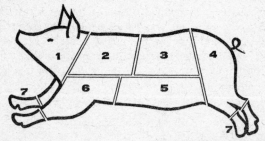

1. Head – *Brawn*.
2. Neck or Fore Loin – *Roast or braise*.
3. Loin – *Roast or chops*.
4. Leg – *Roast or boil*.
5. Belly and Spring – *Boil salted or fresh*.
6. Hand – *Roast or boil*.
7. Trotters – *Braise or boil*.

Potatoes are the classic accompaniments to fish and meat courses and may be fried, roasted, boiled, or baked. They were first introduced into Europe in the sixteenth century from South America. There are many varieties, maturing throughout mid-summer to early autumn. The latter are keeping varieties and if properly stored remain sound throughout the winter and early spring. The varieties may be 'floury', good for baking or mashing; slightly waxy for chips and roasting; and very waxy for salads.

Sweet or *Spanish potatoes* are large, reddish-brown tubers from the climbing plant *Batatas edulis*. They are usually boiled and served mashed.

Potato Flour. See FÉCULE.

Pot-au-Feu. A large deep earthenware casserole or *marmite* which holds the classic boiled beef of France. Contrary to the English tradition the beef is fresh not salt, but both are cooked and served with root vegetables. The broth is served as soup before the beef is eaten. Pot-au-feu is also the name given to the food.

Pot-Herbs. Herbs for culinary use. Also a name given to a mixture of sliced root vegetables with herbs, sold in the north of England for use in broths and stews.

Pot-Roasting (i.e. roast in a pot). The meat or bird is browned first in a deep pot or pan, the lid is put on, and the whole gently simmered with herbs and vegetables to flavour. The meat must be basted frequently during cooking. This is an ideal method for medium-priced cuts of meat. After browning, the meat may be put into a terrine and cooked in the oven. See TERRINE.

Poularde. A hen bird caponized. See CAPON.

Poulette. A velouté sauce finished with an egg liaison, lemon juice, and chopped parsley. Used with veal and sweetbread dishes and broad beans.

Poultry. Domestic birds bred especially for the table, i.e. chicken, duck, goose, guinea fowl, and turkey.

Poussin. See CHICKEN.

Praliné. A confection of almonds and burnt sugar. Praliné is usually crushed or ground before it is added to creams, soufflés, ices, etc. See NOUGAT.

Prawn. A crustacean, of which two or three varieties are sold in England. The English prawn, caught round our shores, is $1\frac{1}{2}$–2 in. long, the Mediterranean prawn 3–4 in., and the Pacific prawn 4–5 in. The shell of each when boiled is bright red and shiny with long whiskers and a horny proboscis. The smaller prawn is sold by the pint or 'picked', i.e. shelled, and frozen. *Dublin Bay prawns* are a different variety, with a hard shell; they resemble a *langoustine* or baby crawfish. The shelled Dublin Bay prawn is also called by its Italian name, SCAMPI.

Preserve. Fruit preserved with sugar. See JAM.

Pretzel. German and Alsatian savoury biscuit baked in the shape of a loose knot and sprinkled with salt. Served with beer.

Profiterole. Small marble of chou pastry. The best known are those filled with chocolate cream and coated with rich chocolate sauce, i.e. *profiteroles au chocolat*.

Provençale (cooking from Provence). The dishes and sauces from this region contain oil, garlic, and tomatoes.

Prune. The dried fruit of a special variety of plum. Prunes are usually soaked before being gently stewed. There is, however, a specially treated packaged prune which does not require a preliminary soaking.

Ptarmigan. A species of grouse found over high ground. The plumage is brown but changes to white in winter. Though once quite common in the shops, ptarmigan is rarely seen nowadays.

Puchero. A Spanish and South American stew of beans, meat, and sausage.

Pudding. The sweet course of a meal; a term generally applied to sweets other than creams and soufflés, e.g. steamed or baked puddings, apple fritters, and so on. Puddings may also be savoury, e.g. beef steak and kidney, beefsteak and oyster. The meat is enclosed in a suet crust in a pudding basin and put to cook in a pan of boiling water. See BLACK PUDDING and WHITE PUDDING.

Pulse. The seeds of a pod-bearing plant. In cookery the name is given to dried vegetables – peas, lentils, beans, etc.

Pumpernickel. Westphalian black bread baked from unbolted rye flour. Pumpernickel is sold in packets very thinly sliced; it is served plain or buttered to eat with sausage.

Pumpkin. A large orange-coloured gourd. In season in the early autumn, pumpkin is the traditional ingredient for pies on Thanksgiving Day. Pumpkin is popular in soups and may also be cooked and served like swede, i.e. boiled and mashed. The flesh is a deep yellow, and the flavour slightly sweet.

Punch. A mixed alcoholic drink, e.g. rum punch, whisky punch, etc. It is said of punch that it is composed of four or five ingredients, strong, sweet, sour, weak, i.e. spirit, sugar, lime or lemon, and water.

Purée. Cooked meat, vegetables, or fruit sieved, beaten, or worked in an electric blender to form a thick cream.

Purslane (*Portulaca oleracea*). An annual herb, the shoots of which can be used in salads. The leaves are fleshy and may be pickled like nasturtium seeds. Not frequently grown nowadays.

Quail. A small game bird in the luxury class. Once very popular for the cold table and now, after a considerable period of time, on the market again. Quail farms, where the birds may be obtained, have been established in England.

Queen Cake. Small cake made of a Victoria sponge mixture and baked in fancy-shaped tins, e.g. spades, hearts, clubs, diamonds.

Queen of Puddings. A favourite pudding of Victorian days which has survived. A layer of strawberry jam is placed in the bottom of a pie-dish, a mixture of breadcrumbs, milk, and egg-yolks poured in, and the whole put in the oven to set. After this the egg-whites are made into a meringue and piled on top, and the pudding returned to the oven to crisp.

Quenelle. A kind of dumpling made with veal, fish, or chicken forcemeat, bound with eggs. These may be poached in special moulds; or the mixture can be shaped in dessert or tea-spoons, before being put into boiling water. After draining they are coated with a cream or *velouté* sauce. The traditional shape is oval.

Quiche. A savoury flan or tart from Lorraine. The pastry is usually *pâte brisée* (short-crust) and the filling a rich egg custard with pieces of crisp bacon and onion.

Quince. The fruit of *Cydonia vulgaris* or common quince. Quince trees are grown principally in private gardens, and mature in late September to early October. The fruit is large, irregularly pear-shaped, and yellow-gold in colour with a grey bloom. Quinces have an exotic yet tart, astringent flavour, and cannot be eaten raw. They are at their best in jellies and conserves.

R

Rabbit. Rabbits are in season from early autumn to February and though classed as game may be bought throughout the year. Wild rabbits have gone out of favour owing to the prevalence of myxomatosis, but in spite of that are still plentiful and make good eating. Ostend or tame rabbit, specially bred for the table, has firm white flesh resembling chicken.

Radish. A summer salad or relish; small bright red roots with a strong peppery taste. Both red and white radishes may be round or tapered. They should be grown quickly, as otherwise they are inclined to be over-hot and tough. The Spanish or black radish is tap-rooted and much larger. It is served unpeeled and sliced as an apéritif or *crudité* to be nibbled before a meal.

Ragout. A meat stew of beef, mutton, veal, etc., which may be either brown or white (usually the former).

Raisin. The dried fruit of a large white grape. Raisins are now sold seeded, i.e. with the pips removed, and are not to be confused with seedless raisins, which are the size of sultanas and like them have no seeds. See MALAGA.

Ramekin or Ramequin. Small fireproof china or glass case, i.e. an individual soufflé case, used for savouries and first courses, e.g. cheese ramekins (small cheese soufflés).

Rare. In cooking, a term applied to the grilling of steaks, to mean underdone.

Rasher. A slice of bacon or raw ham. Rashers are cut on a special slicer in varying thicknesses, each having a number. Nos. 3 to 4 are classed as thin, 5 to 6 medium thick, and 7 thick.

Raspberry. A mid-summer to autumn fruit, raspberries are rich in colour as well as flavour, and they are used in the same ways as strawberries. White raspberries are also grown, though their flavour is not so pronounced.

Ratafia. A macaroon the size of a small button and strongly flavoured with almond. Used for cream sweets and puddings.

Ratafia is also a liqueur flavoured with oil of almonds.

Ratatouille. A dish from Provence: a mixture of aubergines, sweet peppers, courgettes, and tomatoes first fried in olive oil and then stewed gently together until they form a soft, rich mass.

Ravigote. A sauce: chopped tarragon, chervil, and parsley added to an oil and vinegar dressing and worked with hard-boiled egg-yolks. Chopped gherkins and capers are also added. Ravigote is served with cold fish, calf's head, veal, etc. It may also be hot, in which case it consists of a *velouté* or *béchamel* sharpened with lemon juice or white wine with the same herbs added, but without gherkins or capers.

Ravioli. Small squares or rounds of raw PASTA filled with a spinach and cream cheese mixture or a savoury mince. After being simmered in stock or water the ravioli is finished in a rich tomato sauce.

Réchauffé. Literally 're-heated'. Denotes those dishes that are made with cooked meat or poultry, e.g. cottage pie.

Red Mullet. See MULLET.

Reduce. In the culinary sense, to boil down in order to concentrate the flavour and thicken the consistency of a sauce or gravy.

Reform. A sauce: a *poivrade* with a julienne garnish of tongue, egg-white, truffle, mushroom and gherkin. Cutlets reform: a dish in which cutlets are coated with egg and breadcrumbs, fried, and served with the sauce.

Refresh. A term applied to a process which may follow blanching of vegetables and some meats. Once the food has been drained, a cupful or so of cold water is poured over it. In the case of vegetables this 'sets' the colour. Where meat is concerned it helps to clean and wash away any scum, e.g. with brains, sweetbreads, etc.

Relevé. See REMOVE.

Rémoulade. A cold sauce with a base of mayonnaise to which are added chopped tarragon, chervil, and parsley and chopped gherkins and capers. Served with cold fish, eggs, and meat.

Remove or **Relevé.** A term now obsolete but used in Victorian and Edwardian times to denote the main course of a dinner. The remove consists of a joint which is roast, braised or boiled, with potatoes and a vegetable to accompany it. See MENU.

Render. To melt fat down into dripping. This is done by putting the pieces of fat in a roasting tin in a moderate oven until the dripping runs freely and the pieces of fat are brown. The dripping is then strained off. Alternatively the fat may be put into a pan with a small quantity of water and boiled until all the water has evaporated. The fat should be clear and still before it is strained.

Rennet. A substance extracted from the lining membrane of the true stomach of the sucking calf. It is used for coagulating milk in the making of junket and hard cheese. Rennet obtainable from most grocers is suitable for making junket, but rennet for cheese-making can be bought only from dairy suppliers.

Rhubarb. A plant first cultivated for medical purposes. For cooking, rhubarb is at its best in the early spring: the delicate pink stalks are delicious simmered in syrup and served cold with cream. This rhubarb is forced, whereas the later or garden rhubarb is of a more robust colour, firmer in texture, though no less good in flavour. Care must be taken to discard the leaves as they are poisonous.

Rice. Rice is a genus of grass largely cultivated in sub-tropical climates. It requires abundant moisture particularly in the ground. There are several types of grain, originally named after the country or district in which they were grown.

Patna. A long thin grain. For curries, pilaffs, etc.

Carolina. A medium thick grain. For milk puddings and creams.

Spanish Jap or Java. A thick short stubby grain. For risottos and milk puddings.

Italian. Large thick white grains. For risottos.

Ground Rice is rice ground to a medium fine powder, used for puddings, cakes and thickenings.

Wild rice is a different plant; it is grown in America and imported into England. It is something of a luxury.

Ricotta. An Italian curd cheese used, among other things, in the making of ravioli.

Rillettes. *Rillettes de porc* resemble chitterlings in that they are pieces of the small intestine of the pig fried in pork fat. *Rillettes* can also be made from shredded lean and fat pork fried in pork fat with herbs and seasonings. When cold they may be pounded and the paste put down in pots to eat cold as a first course. The making of *rillettes* varies a little according to the district.

Risotto. An Italian dish of rice simmered gently in stock until thick and creamy. The risotto can have various additions such as mushrooms and beef marrow (*Milanese*), tomatoes (*Napolitana*), and so on. All are finished with cheese.

Rissole. A *réchauffé*. Minced meat placed on rounds of short-crust or flaky pastry and folded to form a turnover. They are then fried in deep fat, or may first be coated with egg and breadcrumbs, or rolled in crushed vermicelli. See also CRO-QUETTE.

Rissoler. To brown slowly in fat.

Roast. A course in the MENU after the sorbet and before the *entremets*. The roast is game or poultry served with game chips and a green salad, or nowadays meat.

Roasting. True roasting is done on a spit over an open fire, or on a gas or electric spit. Like grilling, this method uses radiant heat, and as the joint turns, it must be well basted to keep it succulent.

Robert. A piquant sauce made on the base of a *demi-glace* to which white wine and mustard are added. Served with pork fillets, kidneys, or steak.

Rock Salmon. Also called cat fish or rock eel. Sold skinned, it has a slightly pinkish tinge with firm flesh. Much used in fried fish shops.

Rock Salt. See SALT.

Röd Gröd. A Danish sweet. It is made from the juice of red fruit, currants or raspberries, together with a small proportion of the fruit, and thickened with sago. Sometimes served as a soup. *Kissel* (Polish or Russian), with black cherries and currants added to the red fruit, is thickened with arrowroot. Also served as a soup or sweet.

Roe. The reproductive glands of fish. Soft roe or MILT is found in the male, hard roe in the female.

Roll-Mop. Herrings pickled in spiced vinegar. The fish is boned, rolled up with a slice of onion inside, and fastened with a tooth-pick before being packed into jars.

Roly-Poly. Suet crust rolled out, spread with jam or golden syrup, and rolled up like a Swiss roll. The pudding is then boiled or baked.

Roquefort. One of the most famous of the blue-veined cheeses. It is made from ewe's milk, and mouldy breadcrumbs are added to the curd. These play a great part in giving the cheese its unique flavour, as does the limestone of the caves in which it is matured.

Rosemary (*Rosmarinus officinalis*). A tall handsome shrub with aromatic, needle-like leaves and pale blue flowers. It is a herb and can be grown as a hedge for the herb garden. In the kitchen the leaves, fresh or dried, are good put into the roasting-tin with lamb or chicken, or when sautéing potatoes.

Rose-Water. Extract of rose leaves. Sold in chemists' shops. It was at one time used as a flavouring for sponge cakes and creams. Now used mostly for hand and face lotions.

Rouennaise (from Rouen). The most famous speciality is duck rouennaise. The duck is lightly roasted, the carcass pressed to extract the blood, and the sauce made from this with red wine, the liver of the duck, good stock, and *beurre manié*. Rouennaise sauce is a concentrated gravy of red wine, jellied stock, and meat glaze.

Roux. A butter and flour liaison. Used for *béchamel*, *velouté*, and brown sauces. There should be proportionately more butter than flour to make a soft mixture, and so allow the liquid for the sauce to blend easily with the *roux*.

Royale. A savoury custard used as a garnish for clear soup. Egg-white and cream are steamed together until set for white royale, egg-yolk and cream for yellow. When cold and firm the custard is cut into fancy shapes or julienne strips.

Rum. A spirit fermented and distilled from the side products of the manufacture of cane juice into sugar. Rum is largely imported from the West Indies.

Rusk. A light bread dough, shaped and baked slowly until dry and crisp throughout. There are several makes of rusk. See ZWIEBACK.

Russe' à la. Containing beetroot and/or sour cream. Russian salad (vinaigrette) consists of beetroot, apple, potato, cucumber, peas, etc., mixed with fish or meat, and coated with mayonnaise. See also CHARLOTTE RUSSE.

Rust. The underside of a bacon rasher or ham, opposite the rind. This is often hard and strong-flavoured and should be cut away.

Rye. A genus of grass allied to wheat and barley. Rye is an important cereal, though not one much cultivated in England. Rye flour is used largely on the Continent for making breads of all kinds, from black bread to the lighter varieties. Like most grains rye is used in fermentation and distillation, e.g. rye whisky.

S

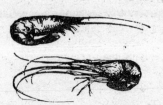

Sabayon. The French version of the Italian ZABAGLIONE, but made with white wine in place of Marsala. The ingredients are whole eggs, sugar, and white wine, and while it is usually served warm as an accompanying sauce to a hot pudding it may also be served in tall glasses as a sweet with ratafias or sponge fingers. A good sabayon should be of a rich mousse-like consistency but not quite so thick as a *zabaglione*.

Sablé. A rich biscuit paste made with as much butter as flour. It can be either sweet, or savoury when it is strongly flavoured with cheese. The paste is usually made up into small biscuits served either plain or sandwiched together with jam or a cheese cream.

Saccharometer. An instrument used to measure by specific gravity the density of sugar in a syrup. It is a necessary piece of equipment for making confectionery, *marrons glacés*, water ices, etc.

Sacristan. A *pâtisserie* made from trimmings of puff pastry. The pastry is rolled and folded two or three times and dusted well with caster sugar in place of flour during the process. It should be chilled before being cut into thin strips 6–7 in. long. These are twisted well and then moved on to a dampened baking-sheet and baked to a good brown in a hot oven, so that the sugar caramelizes slightly. Served with fresh fruit compotes and ice creams, or for tea.

Saddle. A joint of lamb or mutton consisting of the two loins and the connecting vertebrae.

Saffron. Stamens of the saffron crocus (*Crocus sativus*). Used for flavouring and colouring cakes, breads, and savoury rice dishes. As a rule a good pinch is enough for one dish, and it should be soaked in 2–3 tablespoons warm water for half an hour before being added according to the recipe. The stamens are dried and are obtainable at any chemist or big store. As saffron weighs light it is usually sold in very small quantities, e.g. by the drachm.

Sage (*Salvia officinalis*). A herb associated mainly with onion for stuffing goose. Its pungent flavour marries well with the rich meat. The leaves are also used to wrap round cheeses to flavour them. Popular in the eighteenth century as a face wash or bath, a large bunch of sage infused in hot bath water was reputed to have a soothing effect on the nerves.

Sago. A starch that comes from the pith of certain palm trees. Sago has gone out of fashion, but in Victorian and Edwardian times was considered (erroneously) very nourishing and was largely used in invalid and convalescent diets. It is a useful thickener, being rather like arrowroot in its effect, and is used in the Scandinavian sweet RÖD GRÖD. By itself it makes an excellent cream simmered in milk until clear, sweetened when cold, and an appropriate amount of whipped cream folded in. Very good stewed with apple and then smothered with cream when cold.

Saignant (literally 'bloody', very underdone). A term applied to the roasting or grilling of meat and game, especially wild duck.

Saithe. See COAL-FISH.

Salad. A generic term for a dish usually composed of raw greens such as lettuce, cresses, dandelion, chicory, and root vegetables. Salads can also be made with cooked vegetables, fish, meat, cereals, eggs, and fruit. A green salad is usually served with meat, poultry, or game, either to accompany it or immediately afterwards as a separate course. It may also be served with cheese. Many other salads take their place on the menu as an

147

hors-d'œuvre, first, or main course. Salads are mixed with or accompanied by a dressing, either a French dressing for a simple green salad, or, for more elaborate salads, a cream or vinaigrette dressing or mayonnaise sauce.

Salamander. An old-fashioned device used for browning the surface of cooked dishes before the advent of gas and electric grills. It resembled a thick iron plate on a long poker-like handle. The plate was thrust into the fire to get red-hot and then held above the dish until the surface was a rich, even brown. Some salamanders had a stand on which the handle was rested while the dish was being browned, which made matters easier.

Salambô. (A *pâtisserie*, or *petits fours*.) A small chou, well baked, with the top dipped in hot caramel. When the caramel is hard and cold the chou is filled with orange-flavoured whipped cream.

Salami. See CONTINENTAL SAUSAGES.

Sally Lunn. A light teacake served hot, split open, and buttered. Reputed to have been the invention of Sally Lunn of Bath, who made them for the Prince Regent.

Salmagundi. A dish with an intriguing name popular in the seventeenth and eighteenth centuries. In old cookery books it is described as a mixed salad of sliced cooked meats, hard-boiled eggs, beetroot, cucumber, etc., in fact a dish that could appear with advantage on our tables today.

Salmis. A piquant ragout of game or duck. The characteristic of a salmis is that the birds are lightly roasted before being split or jointed, and then immersed in a rich brown sauce flavoured with red wine. The cooking is finished by gentle simmering on the top of the cooker or in the oven for 15–20 minutes. The dish is garnished with croûtons of fried bread.

Salmon. Known as the king of fish. Salmon spend a great part of their life in the sea, but come up large rivers to spawn. They are caught in rivers or netted at the mouth, and the season for prime salmon varies to some extent according to the river, those on the east coast of Scotland usually being the first (e.g. Tay, starts in February). Salmon vary in weight from about 7 to 50 lb., the average being around 10–25 lb. Those around 7 lb. are known as grilse, young fish that have been down to the sea for the first time. Salmon may be cooked whole, or cut in steaks. The flesh is also conserved by drying, smoking, and canning. Served hot, salmon may be accompanied by anchovy butter or hollandaise sauce; cold, by mayonnaise or tartare sauce.

Salmon-Trout (or Sea-Trout). No relation to the salmon, but similar in appearance, with a silvery skin and occasional dark or black spots and pink flesh, and with the same habits of returning to rivers to spawn. At the beginning of the century they were considered inferior to salmon, but nowadays, and perhaps because of the smaller size of the whole fish (around 2½–6 lb.), they are as popular and considered more delicate in flavour. They are best served whole, either hot or cold, with the same accompaniments as salmon.

Salpicon. A mixture of shredded chicken, ham, game, or mushrooms, bound with a brown or white sauce. Can be used as a filling for *bouchées*, *vol-au-vents*, and other dishes.

Sal-Prunella. A form of saltpetre, used to quicken the process of pickling or salting. It should be used in very small quantities.

Salsify. Known as the oyster of the garden, this vegetable is uncommon in markets and little known to the public. It deserves popularity as it is one of the most delicately flavoured vegetables. There are two varieties, the white and the black. The black is known as scorzonera and is undoubtedly the better of the two. Both are grown easily in private gardens. The simplest way to prepare salsify for the table is to scrub the long tapering roots well, then boil them in salted water until tender – about 45–50 minutes. Drain, then rub and peel off the skin (this applies particularly to the scorzonera). Serve with hot melted butter or in a sauce.

Salt (sodium chloride). *Common or kitchen salt* is sold in bags or blocks. *Table salt* is refined to make it easier to pour out of a shaker and less liable to coagulate in damp weather. *Rock or bay salt*: coarse crystals for use in a salt grinder. A coarser and less pure type of this salt is sold as freezing salt for use with ice. See FREEZER.

Saltpetre (nitrate of potash). Used largely in pickling salt beef, tongue etc., combined with common salt.

Samphire. A salt, green, fleshy plant which grows wild on sea marshes and sand dunes, especially in East Anglia. It is sold in market towns along the coast. At its best in May, it is eaten principally as a salad, or pickled in vinegar.

Sandwich. Originally a slice of meat between two pieces of buttered bread. Said to have been invented by the Earl of Sandwich who did not wish to leave the gaming table in order to partake of a full meal. There are now many types of sandwich and a wide variety of fillings.

Sangaree. A West Indian drink made with port and spices and lightly sweetened. It is diluted with crushed ice and laced with brandy. A long rather than a short drink.

Sardine. Small silvery fish caught off the French, Portuguese, and Spanish coasts. It is said that they were first found off Sardinia, hence the name. Sardines are the young of pilchards, and though they are excellent eaten fresh, they cannot be sent long distances without deterioration. For this reason almost everywhere the fish is known only salted or, most frequently, preserved in olive oil and tinned. French-packed sardines were formerly considered the best, owing to the quality of the fish and of the oil, but nowadays they are rivalled by the Portuguese. Sardines lend themselves to many dishes, but especially those for *hors-d'œuvre* and savouries.

Satsuma. A large, particularly juicy variety of tangerine imported into England from Spain; it appears in the shops in mid-November.

Sauce. In a general way the word 'sauce' implies a seasoned liquid served with, or on, food. The origin of the word is from 'salt', though sauces can now be sweet or savoury. They can be made from the liquid in which the food they are to accompany has been cooked, and thickened by various means – e.g. butter, flour, and egg-yolks. Alternatively they may be made separately and served as an accompaniment to grills, roasts, vegetables, and the like. The liquid can be a meat stock or milk according to the type of sauce. See also AÏOLI, BÉARNAISE, BÉCHAMEL, BERCY, BIGARADE, BLANCHE, BORDELAISE, BREAD SAUCE, BROWN, CHAUDFROID, DEMI-GLACE, ESPAGNOLE, HOLLANDAISE, MAYONNAISE, MORNAY, POIVRADE, POULETTE, RAVIGOTE, REFORM, RÉMOULADE, ROBERT, ROUENNAISE, SOUBISE, SUPRÊME, TARTARE, VELOUTÉ, VINAIGRETTE.

Bottled sauces such as Worcester sauce, tomato ketchup, and others with proprietary names are really CONDIMENTS, and should be used sparingly and only for certain dishes.

Saucepan. Essentially a medium to small pan, about $4\frac{1}{2}$–5 in. deep; this allows for easy stirring without the liquid splashing over the side. Its narrow diameter means that a comparatively small surface of the sauce is exposed to the air, so that if the sauce stands for a short time only a small amount of skin is likely to form. Saucepans have lids, with the exception of those intended for milk which have sloping sides and a lip for easy pouring. They are made in various metals and finishes – aluminium, tin-lined copper, stainless steel, enamel, enamelled iron.

Sauerkraut (French, choucroute). To quote a Victorian cookery book: 'A variety of pickled cabbage so dear to many of our travelling classes. Cold meat and pickled cabbage are usually considered quite good enough for a wayside luncheon, just as in Germany Sour-Crout is esteemed as an appetizing accompaniment to plain food.' Sauerkraut is the hard, white drum-head cabbage sliced wafer-thin, then soured or fermented in brine from 4 to 6 weeks. Nowadays it is more convenient to buy it ready prepared from a Delicatessen shop or in tins. It should be blanched before use (see BLANCH) and then braised or stewed. A classic accompaniment to goose, boiled pork, sausage, or any rich meat. A favourite dish is CHOUCROUTE GARNIE. Sauerkraut is considered wholesome.

Sausage. Finely minced or ground meat mixed with a proportion of crumb or rusk or starch of some kind, lightly seasoned, and cased in gut. The meat is usually pork, though beef sausages have become popular and are a little cheaper. See also CONTINENTAL SAUSAGES.

Sauté. Food cooked as a sauté should be of good quality or young – e.g. sirloin of beef, veal cut from leg or loin, or a chicken weighing no more than $2\frac{1}{2}$ lb. Sweetbreads, lamb's and calf's kidneys, and liver may also be sautéd. The food is browned carefully in butter, or a mixture of oil and butter. After it is taken from the pan a sauce is made according to the recipe. The food is then replaced and cooked in the sauce. The pan should be wide and shallow to contain the food easily and to allow for quick reduction. If a proper sauté pan or stewpan is not at hand, use a frying-pan with an improvised lid such as a plate. In this way the gravy or sauce will be properly reduced. In a finished sauté the liquid should be just sufficient to coat the meat or poultry, and not too highly reduced so that it is harsh or over-concentrated in flavour. Depending on what food is being used the sauté may be cooked on top of the stove throughout or, alternatively, after the initial cooking in butter, put into the oven with a lid on the pan. When cooking chicken in this way the initial cooking in butter, or oil and butter, is slower than when using meat (such as beef) or offal. If using oil and butter heat the pan first, put in the oil, and after a second or two add the butter; then continue according to the recipe.

Sauté Pan. Similar to a deep frying-pan but with straight sides. Used to sauté meat or poultry.

Savarin. A cake made with a light rich yeast dough, which after baking is soaked with a Kirsch- or rum-flavoured syrup. The characteristic of a savarin is that it is baked in a special ring mould with a rounded top (i.e. distinct from a border mould). When finished the centre may be filled with fruit, e.g. *savarin Montmorency*, filled with cherries and flavoured with Kirsch; or *savarin Chantilly*, filled with *crème Chantilly*. See BABA.

Saveloy. A small sausage sold already cooked. The name is a corruption of *cervelas* as originally brains, usually pigs', were the main ingredient. Now the sausages are generally made with pork or pig's head, well flavoured with herbs and spices, and lightly smoked. The best saveloys come from Italy.

Savoie. Mountainous district in France, well known for dairy produce, game, and fresh-water fish, and also for *pâtisserie*. Famous too for a type of sponge cake, *biscuit de Savoie*. Dishes cooked *à la savoyarde* have eggs, milk, potatoes, and Gruyère cheese as the main ingredients; for example, an omelet, *œufs sur le plat*, or sliced potatoes baked in good stock with cheese and butter.

Savory (*Satureia montana* and *S. hortensis*). An aromatic herb useful in any stuffing. It has a slight flavour of sage but is more delicate, and is the herb which should be used with broad beans. Chop a few of the leaves and add them to the cooked beans with a good knob of butter. There are two kinds of savory: summer savory, an annual, and winter savory, a perennial. Both are easy to cultivate.

Savoury. A small piquant morsel served as the last course in the dinner menu. The object of the savoury is to clean the palate after the sweet course in preparation for the port to follow. Classic savouries are: ANGELS ON HORSEBACK, cheese soufflé, WELSH RAREBIT, etc.

Savoy. See CABBAGE.

Scald. To plunge any food into boiling water to harden it and facilitate peeling.

Scallion. See ONION and SHALLOT.

Scallop. One of the best of the shellfish. Clean, handsome, and delicately flavoured, scallops are at their best in January and February. The firm white nut of flesh has an orange-coloured roe or 'tongue' attached, surrounded by a fringe or beard. This should be removed when the scallop is opened as it usually contains grit. Fishmongers sell scallops opened, and with the deep shell on request. Should they arrive in the kitchen unopened, however, the best method of opening them is to put them into a moderately hot oven for 5–6 minutes. They can then be opened easily and the beard removed. Scallops may be cooked in several ways; the simplest is the best in order to preserve the delicate flavour. Like all shellfish they should not at any stage be allowed to boil hard because this turns them into hard pieces of rubber instead of tender morsels.

Scalloped. A term derived from the shell of the scallop. As a method of cooking it is similar to *au gratin*, but the food, sauce, and/or garnishes are cooked and finished in the scallop shell. Dishes completed in this way are popular as first courses, so much so that scallop shells in china or silver are obtainable.

Scampi. Basically scampi are Mediterranean prawns, but any large prawn, Pacific or Dublin Bay, may be classed as scampi. In England they are most easily obtainable frozen. Dublin Bay prawns are packed in three different sizes, ready shelled and prepared for cooking. They are more tender and delicate in both texture and flavour than the ordinary prawns and lend themselves to many ways of cooking. See PRAWN.

Schnitzel. See WIENER SCHNITZEL.

Scone. Originated in Scotland. Scones are made of a farinaceous material – white or brown wheat-flour, oatmeal, barley, or potato – combined with sour milk or buttermilk. A scone proper is a three-cornered cake or farl, made by cutting a round, roughly 8 inches in diameter, into four. They may be oven-baked, or cooked on a girdle.

Scorzonera. See SALSIFY.

Scotch Woodcock. A rich savoury custard poured over hot buttered toast, spread with pounded anchovies or anchovy paste. Served hot.

Sea Bream. See BREAM.

Sea-Kale. A delicious vegetable renowned for its delicacy of flavour. Though it grows wild around English coasts, it is better known when forced and blanched, in the same way as chicory, to be eaten in mid-winter. The stems are pure white, about 6–8 in. long, with a grey-green tip. To cook, tie it in bundles and boil them in salted water about 20–30 minutes. Well drained and served hot on a napkin with melted butter or hollandaise sauce sea-kale forms a separate course in the menu, like asparagus. See CHARD.

Sea-Trout. See SALMON-TROUT.

Semolina. Grains of wheat left after 'bolting' (a method of sifting flour). Used mainly for puddings, moulds, soufflés, and so on, it can also be used for bread, and for gnocchi in place of maize meal (*polenta*).

Sesame Seed. Small brown seeds of a herbaceous semi-tropical plant. Used to make oil, and also *halva*, a sweetmeat from the Middle East.

Shad. A salt-water fish which migrates to rivers and lakes like the salmon. A small to medium-sized fish, it runs up to 10 lb. in weight, and is reddish silvery in colour. It is better known on the Continent and in America than in England, and is highly esteemed. One of the best ways of cooking it is in the American fashion – 'planked' shad. The fish is split and put on to a thin plank, or shingle, of pinewood, and set near the fire or under the grill to brown the top. It is then put on the heat so that the under side of the fish will cook and the wood burn slowly round it. It is a piece of cookery for a camp-fire or range, but can be done on (or under) an electric grill. Shad roe is also a delicacy, and may be fried or grilled rather in the manner of cod's roe.

Shaddock. Now generally called grapefruit. Shaddocks were so called after a Captain Shaddock who introduced the fruit from China into the West Indies. Shaddocks are sometimes known as pomeloes.

Shallot. A small onion with a mild and delicate flavour. Shallots, when planted, multiply into three or four bulbs, each about ½ oz. in weight, and are easily recognizable by their reddish-brown outside skin, and slightly purple streaked flesh. They are valuable in the kitchen not only for their flavour but for their size when only a small amount of onion is required. Shallots can also be cooked whole, plainly boiled, and tossed in butter or parsley, or glazed, as a garnish or accompanying vegetable. Shallots are sometimes called scallions, especially in the north of England.

Shashlik. See KABAB.

Sherbet. An iced drink, common in the Middle East, frozen to a semi-solid consistency, and flavoured with flowers and fruits – rose petals, violets, etc. In the U.S. a sherbet is a variety of water ice.

Sherry. The most famous of the Spanish wines. Sherry is a fortified wine, i.e. brandy is added to it at a certain stage of fermentation. There is no such thing as a vintage sherry; sherry is the result of expert blending of the harvest of several years. There are several types varying from the very dry, to the rich sweet dessert sherries. South Africa also produces good sherries which are less expensive than the Spanish. See FLAMBER.

Shortbread. A rich shortcake associated with Scotland, made of butter and plain flour in equal, or near equal, proportions and well sweetened. The paste is pressed on to wooden moulds, and then turned out on to thick baking-sheets to cook to a pale brown. The shortbread can be decorated before it is baked with candied peel and comfits to taste. Always made for New Year and other festive occasions in Scotland.

Shortening. A fat (lard or vegetable) which when rubbed into flour makes it crisp and pliable when baked. It contains no liquid, unlike butter, and this gives the 'short' texture.

Shrewsbury Cake. Akin to a rich shortbread.

Shrimp. There are two kinds of shrimp, the brown and the pink. The brown are true shrimp, and this colour only applies to the outer shell. The pink shrimp is often a young prawn, and may be recognized by a serrated horny protuberance in the front of the head. Many shrimps are today sold ready shelled, or 'picked', in frozen or potted form. They are considered to have a more delicate flavour and texture than PRAWNS.

Shrub. A drink or cordial made from fruit juice, syrup, and rum or brandy. Akin to sherbert, from which the name is probably derived. Popular in the nineteenth century.

Sieve. A term given to a hoop of wood across which is stretched fine or coarse wire, or nylon. The latter replaces the old-fashioned hair sieve. Sieves are used to purée raw or cooked foods; hair or nylon sieves are used especially for fruit or anything acid which might be spoiled by contact with wire. Mouli-sieves, a proprietary brand, are much in use in the modern kitchen. They are quickly adjustable to a fine or coarse mesh, easy to clean, and quick to use. See STRAINER.

Sild. The young of herring and the same as brisling. Sild, like brisling, are bought tinned or smoked in England.

Simmer. To cook foods in liquids and sauces. The liquid should be just below boiling-point (195° F.) so that the surface movement is very slight.

Simnel. A rich fruit cake from Lancashire, sandwiched and decorated with marzipan and finished with icing. Traditionally baked for Mothering Sunday in mid-Lent.

Sippets. Name given to small triangular pieces of crisp toast arranged round a dish of mince. These make a pleasant contrast to the soft mince.

Skate. An excellent fish, though hideous (one of the reasons why it does not appear whole on the fishmonger's slab). Apart from the liver (and this is obtainable only where the fish is caught) the only parts eaten are the side pieces or 'wings', which weigh 1–2 lb. each. The dark skin is removed by the fishmonger. To cook, it is usual to cut the wings into thick fingers right through the semi-gristle which forms the bones. Skate may be fried in batter (popular in fried-fish shops) or poached and finished with black butter (*beurre noir*), a popular dish in France. Skate is caught largely off the Cornish coasts, and fishermen favour the practice of hanging the wings in the sun for 2–3 days before they are cooked.

Skewer. Skewers are made in various sizes, and in different metals, or in wood, which a butcher uses. As the name implies they may skewer meat or joints together, or be used to impale various meats for grilling. Shapes vary slightly, the commonest being the twisted skewer made to hold the meat firmly in place. Thin round skewers are more suitable for delicate meats, as they are less inclined to tear the flesh (skewering a kidney, for example, to keep it flat while grilling). Skewers with an edge are best for kababs and brochettes, as the edge helps to prevent the food from slipping round. Other skewers which at one time were much in vogue were ATTELETTES, used for fixing garnishes in place on cold dishes for a buffet, or simply for sticking into hams and galantines as an added attraction.

Skillet. An American term for a frying-pan.

Slake. In cooking a word usually applied to the mixing of arrowroot or cornflour with a small quantity of cold water before adding to a liquid for thickening. The proportions for mixing are one heaped teaspoonful of arrowroot, etc. to two tablespoons of cold water.

Slaw. See COLE SLAW.

Sloe. The fruit of blackthorn, which grows wild in the hedgerows and bears fruit around September. A sloe resembles a damson but is smaller, harder, and more sour in flavour. Little used in the kitchen, but better known for making sloe gin. Sometimes mixed with elderberries for making jelly to give additional pectin and flavour.

Smelt. Known as the cucumber of the sea, as it both smells and tastes of cucumber. Smelts are small (about 5–6 in. long), delicate little fish, almost translucent in appearance. They are not often seen nowadays but before the Second World War were sold by the dozen, packed in shallow wooden boxes because of their fragile nature. They are usually fried or baked with butter and lemon.

Smörgåsbord (Scandinavian). Open sandwiches topped with many varieties of fish, meat, eggs, vegetables, and fruit combinations. Smörgåsbord may be almost a meal in itself, but small open sandwiches may be made for *hors-d'œuvre* and snacks.

Snail. Edible snails are imported from France, those from Burgundy being reputed to be the best. These snails, like most edible snails, are fed on vine leaves. They are a little tricky to prepare at home, and so it is really wiser to eat them in a good restaurant where the chef thoroughly understands the method of cooking.

Snipe. A very small and much prized game bird similar to a woodcock. The season runs from September throughout the winter months. To cook, the birds are plucked, and left undrawn, and the head may be left on. The long beak, a feature of the snipe, is then thrust under and through the thighs (the legs are crossed first), in order to truss the bird. According to connoisseurs, snipe should 'fly through the kitchen': the best method being to roast them in a Dutch oven in front of the kitchen fire for 2–3 minutes on each side. Nowadays they can be spit-roasted, which answers as well. Those with no spit available can set the birds on a grid in a roasting-tin, rub them well with butter, and roast them 5–6 minutes in a very hot oven.

Serve, with their juices, on toast, and with game chips to accompany.

Socle. Cooked pounded rice moulded into the desired shape (round, oval, etc.), and sometimes covered with silver paper. A socle was used to mount *pièces froides*, and lift them from the surface of the dish to make a good presentation. It was not intended to be eaten. Little used nowadays, and then only for formal banquets.

Soda (Bicarbonate). Used mostly as a raising agent in cakes such as fruit, ginger, and dripping cakes. It also has a darkening quality and is reputed to keep a cake moister than if a baking powder is used. For scones and soda breads it is also added as a raising agent if sour milk is used for mixing. If sweet milk is used then cream of tartar (acid) should be added with the soda. At times a pinch of soda is put into the cooking water of green vegetables to preserve the colour and to soften the vegetables, e.g. old peas. A pinch can also be put with sour plums and rhubarb when stewing.

Sole. The best of the flat fish. The flesh is firm and white, and delicate in flavour. There are three or four varieties, the best being the Dover or black sole; it is narrower than the other kinds and has dark grey-black skin on the upper side and a white under side. Next in quality is the lemon sole, slightly less expensive than the black with a rich brown upper skin. Finally there are the Torbay or witches, but in comparison the flesh is poor and the whole fish on the bony side.

Sorbet (French for sherbet). In Victorian days a sorbet, or water ice, usually lemon, was served between the entrée and roast to refresh and clean the palate before continuing the dinner. Now served only at formal dinners. See MENU.

Sorrel. A herb little cultivated in England, but much used on the Continent. Acid and fresh-tasting, it is delicious made into a purée to serve with eggs, rich meats, or veal – it is the classic accompaniment of a FRICANDEAU. Mixed with spinach it makes an excellent soup, *potage de santé*. Sorrel grows wild as a weed in England, but this is a little too coarse and acid for kitchen use.

Soubise. Either a purée of onions mixed into a thick BÉCHA-MEL sauce, i.e. a soubise purée served with roast mutton, or the same purée mixed into a coating *béchamel* for serving over eggs, fish, etc. A soubise can also be a stuffing – onion purée beaten into rice, the whole well cooked, then sieved and bound with an egg-yolk, e.g. for veal Orloff.

Souchet. A fish broth well flavoured with onions and thickened with potatoes. It resembles an Irish stew made with fish in place of the meat.

Soufflé. The chief ingredients of a soufflé are eggs, but essenti-ally eggs that are separated, the white being whipped to a firm snow before incorporation with the rest of the ingredients. Soufflés may be hot or cold. Those that are hot are composed of cheese, vegetable purées, fish, and so on, bound with a thin *béchamel* sauce before the egg-yolks are beaten in. Hot sweet soufflés have a slightly different base (see PASTRY CREAM), but are generally baked (and served) in a special ovenproof china or glass dish or case. A good soufflé should rise 2 or more inches above the edge of the dish and therefore a band of paper is always tied round the dish before the mixture is turned into it. For a hot soufflé the uncooked mixture should not come above the edge of the dish; for a cold soufflé it must give the appear-ance of having risen, so the dish should be filled to about $\frac{1}{2}$–1 in. above the edge before it is left to set. Cold sweet soufflés are also composed of milk and cream in addition to the eggs, and set with gelatine.

Soup. One of the most important items on the menu. Soup is basically a liquid which precedes solid food, though it can be a meal in itself. In its best and most concentrated form it is a con-sommé, a clear, double-distilled broth. Then come the bisques, fish creams requiring skill and care in making; then the vege-table purées, and creams; and finally the broths. A broth is a strong meat extract from bones, to which vegetables and some cereals (rice and barley) are added for thickening. Long simmering is essential, and these are the soups which really are a meal in themselves. Fish broths also come in this category. Soups are designed to act as a stimulant to the digestion before a meal, though there are those who declare that there is no sense in putting good food on to a swamp. However that may be, there is no doubt that a good soup does invite the digestive juices, and set the pace for the courses that follow. A curious anomaly is that soup is always spoken of as being eaten, not drunk.

Souse. To steep, and to cook in a marinade composed largely of vinegar and/or wine. Applies mainly to fish and calf's head, e.g. soused herrings.

Soya. Soya or soy flour and soy sauce are both made from the soya bean. Soya flour has a high percentage of protein and during the war years was used in bread-making and as a filler for sausages to help build up the protein content. An extract of the bean is soy sauce, a condiment much used in Chinese cooking, and also as the base of bottled sauces such as Worcester sauce.

Spaghetti. One of the Italian PASTAS. Spaghetti is a thin fine rod, cut into lengths of about a foot. When it is to be cooked, it should not be broken up but gently introduced into near-boiling, well-salted water and curled round the interior of the saucepan. Like all pasta spaghetti should only be simmered, for if allowed to boil hard it tends to toughen. It takes approximately 12 minutes to cook, and should break easily when pierced by the thumb-nail. After draining, rinse in hot water, return to the pan, and toss over the heat with a good knob of butter. The spaghetti is then ready for serving plain or mixed with a sauce, tomato, cheese, and so on.

Spanish Potato. See POTATO.

Spatchcock. A term applied to small birds split down the back,

162

before being grilled. The back-bone is trimmed a little, the bird flattened, and the whole kept in place with one or two small skewers (i.e. spitted). Grill in the usual manner, well brushed with melted butter. Serve plain with watercress and a gravy or devil sauce to accompany. Eels may be treated in the same way but here the term is changed to 'spitchcock'.

Spatula. A wooden spoon, flat on both sides (i.e. without a bowl). It is ideal for stirring sauces and creamed mixtures.

Spice. Under this heading come most of the condiments in use in our kitchens today. All of them should be employed sparingly to enhance the flavour of the dishes to which they are added. As with herbs, too much will spoil a dish completely. What should also be borne in mind is that certain spices will only marry with certain foods. The following spices are those that are most in use today: ALLSPICE; CINNAMON; CLOVES; GINGER; MACE; NUTMEG; white and black PEPPERCORNS.

Spinach. A leaf vegetable. Four different types of vegetable are classed as spinach, although they are not all of the same family. (1) The true or summer spinach with a short cropping season; a winter variety is also grown. (2) Spinach beet or perpetual spinach, in season throughout the year. (3) Sea-kale beet, of which the leaves are eaten as spinach and the stems cooked as SEA-KALE (see CHARD). (4) New Zealand spinach, with a small dark green almost glaucous leaf, but with little flavour of spinach. Summer spinach is perhaps the most delicately flavoured, with a large, bright green, tender leaf, and is the best type of spinach to use, blanched, as a salad. Besides being a good vegetable to accompany many entrées and roasts, spinach also makes soups, creams, and fritters.

Split Pea. Dried pea split in two at the natural division. Split peas must be well soaked before they are cooked, and they are usually served as a purée.

Sprat. Small silvery fish 3–4 in. long. They are the young of herring and when eaten freshly caught are very good. Like a herring they should be a bright silver when fresh, and red about the eyes. Inexpensive fish, they are best grilled and served with a mustard butter, or rolled in seasoned flour and deep fat fried. They are also smoked; see BRISLING and SILD.

Spurtle. A wooden stick used traditionally for stirring porridge and still obtainable in Scotland.

Squab. A term applied to a young plump pigeon, specially bred for the table.

Squash (American). A member of the gourd family, *Cucurbita*. There are both edible (see PUMPKIN) and ornamental squashes.

Squash is also a commercially prepared fruit drink, orange, lemon, etc. The juice is bottled ready for dilution. Squash can be made at home from fresh fruit juice with the addition of tartaric acid to preserve it.

Squid. See OCTOPUS.

Steak. A slice of meat, usually beef. The better-quality cuts, e.g. fillet steak, rump steak, are for grilling or frying; buttock or chuck for stewing or braising. See BEEF.

Steaming. A method of cookery by moist heat used principally for puddings, meat and fish creams, and some vegetables. A steamer is in two parts: the bottom a large saucepan which is half-filled with boiling water; and a top, which fits on to the bottom pan, with holes in the bottom through which the steam can pass and a lid. Steamer tops can be bought in varying sizes to fit any saucepan. The water in the bottom half is kept at a steady boil for the given time and must be replenished with boiling water when necessary. Cover the food in the steamer with paper or foil and put on the lid; avoid removing it during the steaming time as this will cause condensation and loss of heat. A steamer can be improvised by placing the covered bowl or mould containing the raw food on a folded piece of paper in a roomy saucepan. Boiling water is poured in to come half-way up the sides, and the pan covered with a lid. It should boil steadily, but not violently, for the given time.

Sterlet. A small species of STURGEON found in Russia. It is much esteemed for its flavour, and its roe gives the finest CAVIAR.

Stew. A basic method of cooking food (meat, fish, vegetables, fruit) in water or stock. A stew may be either brown or white. For a brown stew the meat is browned before vegetables and liquid are added. In a white stew the meat is put straight into cold water and when it boils the vegetables are added. Generally beef is used for a brown stew, while mutton or lamb makes a white stew, e.g. Irish stew. A stew needs long slow cooking; the temperature should not rise above simmering point (190° F.).

Stewpan. Like a saucepan but shallower; approximately 3–4 in. deep. Has a lid and sometimes double handles, particularly on the bigger pans, for ease in lifting. Convenient for braising, provided the handles are ovenproof.

Stilton. A semi-hard blue-veined cheese, one of the most famous of the English cheeses. The cheese is drum-shaped and should not be cut, but scooped out from the centre. A little port may be poured on to it and left to soak into the cheese. White Stilton is also available.

Stock. 'A liquid or jelly containing the juices and soluble parts of meat and certain vegetables extracted by cooking for the purpose of making soups, gravies or sauces', to quote from a Victorian cook book. This is a broad general definition; the stock is varied according to the purpose it is required for. Special stock should be made for a consommé, and stock made from sole bones should be used for bisque or *velouté* sauce. But good stock suitable for everyday use can be made from very little; the secret is long slow simmering, up to 4 or 5 hours and even longer. The ingredients, bones, vegetables, etc., may be browned or used as they are, according to whether a brown or white stock is required. After water (usually two thirds of the amount of solid ingredients), half a dozen peppercorns, and a good pinch of salt have been added, it should be brought slowly to the boil, any scum that rises to the surface removed, and then allowed to simmer for the prescribed time. The lid of the pan should be left on, or half on and half off to allow for some evaporation. It is important, especially when bone stock is being made, that the contents should be kept simmering, or at most gently boiling during the cooking. If allowed to boil hard the liquid will be thick and cloudy-looking. As a general rule, stock should be allowed to reduce by at least one third before it is strained. If good fresh bones and meat have been used, more water may be added to make a second stock. When quite cold it will be easy to remove any caked fat from the surface of the strained stock. Good stock should keep for about a week, but if the weather is warm boil it up every second or third day. The more concentrated the stock is, the better it will keep.

Strainer. An important piece of kitchen equipment. Conical or Chinese strainers, made of stainless steel, aluminium or medium to fine mesh tin, are used principally for straining sauces. Gauze strainers are much finer and are sometimes used in place of a tammy cloth. See TAMMY. Bowl strainers in wire or nylon are used for sifting flour, straining small quantities of vegetables, or puréeing fruit for sauces.

Strawberry. A favourite summer and early autumn fruit. There are several varieties, all of which grow in most soils. The majority fruit from early June to late July, but other 'remontant' or perpetuals will give two crops, one in early summer, and another in September which under favourable conditions will last until the end of October. Strawberries are best eaten raw or made into jam. They contain little PECTIN.

Strudel. Usually a sweet or cake, though savoury strudels are excellent and popular. A strudel is composed of a sheet of wafer-thin pastry made from the finest possible flour, water, and a small amount of egg. The whole is beaten together in order to make the paste as elastic as possible, and is then pulled out on a floured cloth until, it is said, print can be read through it. The surface is covered with the chosen ingredients: apple and dried fruit, cherries, cream cheese, and so on for a sweet strudel; cabbage and egg; cooked fish and cauliflower, for example, for a savoury. Tilt the cloth gently from you and the strudel will form a roll. This is then tipped on to a buttered baking-sheet and baked in a hot oven. Cream or various sauces may accompany strudels, but directions are generally given in the recipe.

Stuffing. A mixture of ingredients, chopped or minced and spiced (e.g. sausage meat, minced veal or pork, herbs, rice, breadcrumbs, and a wide variety of vegetables). Essentially stuffing is a seasoning for flavouring meat, poultry, or game, and it is introduced into any handy crevice or pocket in the meat before it is cooked. Where this is not possible, in jugged hare for example, the stuffing is shaped into 'marbles', coated with egg and crumbs, and fried separately to accompany the dish. Stuffing is also known as farce, or forcemeat.

Sturgeon. The royal sturgeon belongs properly to Russia, though it is caught from time to time off English coasts. Any fish unlucky enough to deserve this fate is presented to the reigning monarch, hence the term royal. The sturgeon is an almost prehistoric-looking fish, horny and dragon-like, with a long snout. It grows to enormous size, up to 18 ft long, and is celebrated chiefly for its roe, which is made into CAVIAR. The flesh is close and thick, resembling meat rather than fish; it is obtainable smoked in England. The bladders of the fish are gelatinous and are made into isinglass. Sturgeons, like salmon, spend part of their lives in the sea, returning up the rivers each year to spawn. See STERLET.

Succotash. A cream of sweetcorn served as an accompaniment to meat or poultry. Sometimes mixed with lima beans, and originally an American–Indian dish.

Sucking Pig. A piglet 4–5 weeks old. After being scalded and cleaned the piglet is stuffed and roasted whole. This dish is generally reserved for festivals and holidays, e.g. Christmas.

Suédoise. A term usually applied to a fruit purée set with gelatine and moulded. The fruit used is generally stone fruit – apricots, plums, or apples. It may be served with cream or custard.

Suer (French for to sweat). A cooking method applied to certain white meats (chicken or veal) to whiten the flesh and draw the juices prior to cooking, and also to diced vegetables (*mirepoix*) to be used for braising. Both meat and vegetables are placed in a heavy pan, the bottom of which is lined with pieces of bacon fat or a little butter. The lid is tightly closed and the pan set on a slow heat for 7–10 minutes, after which the other ingredients are added according to the recipe.

Suet. The fat which lies round the kidneys in beef and mutton. The texture is different from that of ordinary fat, being firm, dry, and non-greasy to handle. Beef suet is considered the finest and may be rendered down for deep-fat frying, or for puddings and pastry. If bought from the butcher it should be freed from all membranes before being chopped finely, with a sprinkling of flour to prevent sticking. An old-fashioned practice to keep suet fresh and sweet for a few days was to bury a lump in the flour-bin. If rendered down into a hard white block of dripping it will keep for some time. Ready-prepared shredded suet may now be bought in packets for puddings, pies, and pastry. See RENDER.

Sugar. A sweet substance extracted from many plants, principally the sugar cane and sugar beet. There are many different types of sugar.

(1) BROWN
Barbados. Dark brown, almost black in colour, soft, and moist. Best for ginger and fruit cakes raised by baking soda.
Demerara. Honey-coloured crystals. For table use. Can be sprinkled over bread doughs, ham (which is to be browned), or whenever a good crust is required.
Sand, or Soft Sugar. Pale brown, like damp sand – used for cakes.
Candy. Large crystals from string sugar. Principally used to sweeten coffee.

Foot. Raw sugar containing a large proportion of molasses. Rather like Barbados, but coarser.

(2) WHITE

Granulated. Refined sugar but, as its name implies, coarse in texture. The cheapest of refined sugars and used for general sweetening purposes.

Caster. Very fine granules, used principally for cake-making, puddings, and table use.

Icing. Powdered sugar used for glacé icing; i.e. mixed with syrup or water for icing cakes. Also used mixed with egg-white to make a hard, white icing for wedding and birthday cakes (royal icing).

Loaf. Refined sugar compressed into lumps for table use. In a broken form it is the best sugar for preserving. It is also the best sugar to use to obtain a clear syrup.

Sultana. The dried fruit of a small white seedless grape. Fresh sultana grapes are imported into England in the late summer and are pleasantly acid.

Summer Pudding. An English pudding which is made in a basin lined with slices of bread and filled with a mixture of stewed soft fruit, e.g. red or black currants, raspberries, with plenty of sweetened juice, to soak the bread. It is lightly pressed and left overnight, then turned out and served chilled with cream.

Sundae (American). An ice cream served in a coupe glass with a fruit or nut sauce poured over it.

Suprême. The breast and wing fillet removed in one piece from each side of a chicken carcass.

Suprême is also a word used to indicate a dish that is cooked and presented in a special way. It belongs to *haute cuisine* and implies that only the finest materials are used. Thus one can have a suprême of sole or of sweetbreads as well as of chicken.

Suprême sauce is a *velouté* sauce made with good veal or chicken stock and finished with a higher proportion of cream and egg-yolks than an ordinary *velouté*.

Swede. A species of turnip. Swedes are much larger, firmer, and less watery than turnips, and have a creamy yellow flesh. They are an excellent winter vegetable, cut into pieces and boiled. They can be finished with a cheese sauce, or mashed with butter and seasoned well with black pepper.

Sweetbread. One of the offals. There are two kinds of sweetbread: throat (thymus gland), and pancreas. The former are small and suitable for *fricassées* and fillings in *vol-au-vent* and *bouchée* cases. The latter are larger, about 4–6 in. long, and used to be sold by the pair, but now by the pound. Sweetbreads are a delicate food, easily digested, and they lend themselves to cooking in many ways. A certain amount of preparation is essential. First the sweetbreads must be well soaked in lightly salted water for upwards of 12 hours and the water changed two or three times. They should then be blanched with a slice of lemon in the water, and any fibrous matter or gristle removed. After this they may be pressed lightly until completely cold. They are then ready for further cooking.

Sweetcorn. See INDIAN CORN.

Sweet and Sour. Something that is both sharp and sweet. It became known when Chinese cooking came to the fore in Europe. Sweet and sour is a favourite sauce with pork and fish. The sweet may be honey or sugar, and the sour, vinegar; the whole well seasoned with soy.

Sweet Potato. See POTATO.

Swiss Chard. A variety of spinach beet; see CHARD.

Swiss Roll. A sponge cake baked in a shallow tin or paper case, spread with jam, and rolled up while still warm.

Syllabub. A concoction popular in the eighteenth century, made of cream and wine (sherry and/or white wine), and usually flavoured with lemon. Served cold in individual glasses. Now coming back into fashion.

Syrup. A mixture of sugar and water. The best sugars to use are (a) lump, (b) granulated as these will give a clear syrup. Stock syrup is so called because it can be made and kept ready for general use. Use no more than $\frac{1}{4}$ pint of water for dissolving 1 lb.

sugar; this is sufficient to work with ease and obviates lengthy boiling to reach a given temperature.

Degrees of sugar boiling on Thermometer reading

Short thread	220° F. Butter creams, ices, sabayon
Long thread or feather	230° F.
Soft ball	240° F. Fondant and frosting
Hard crack	325° F. Dipping fruit
Caramel	380°–90° F. Flavouring sauces
Black Jack (burnt caramel)	400° F. and over. Used for colouring, e.g. gravy browning

Tabasco. A commercially prepared sauce made from specially matured hot peppers. For use with shellfish, etc.

Tagliatelle. Strips of PASTA about 1–1½ in. wide.

Tahina. A paste made from sesame seeds and sold in jars at stores or Delicatessens specializing in Middle Eastern groceries. The paste may be mixed with a lentil purée and olive oil, and eaten with bread dipped into it as a first course.

Tamarind. The fruit of *Tamarindus indica*, the tamarind tree, is used for making conserve or chutney and in certain curries. The dried tamarind (amyli) imported into England from India may be infused in a small quantity of water and added to the curry sauce as a 'sour sweet'. The pulp of the fruit is dark brown like that of dates, but more fibrous. The flavour, although slightly sweet, is acrid.

Tammy. To tammy is to wring a sauce or soup through a cloth, to ensure perfect smoothness and to give a high gloss by emulsification. A tammy cloth is made of rough-textured woollen cloth similar to coarse flannel.

Tangerine. See ORANGE.

Tapioca. A starch extracted from the roots of the cassava plant. Tapioca prepared for the market is composed of large rough granules which when simmered in milk or water become transparent and jelly-like. Tapioca is used like SAGO.

Tarama or **Taramasalata.** Popular in Greece and Turkey, this is a *pâté* or paste made of smoked cod's roe. The roe is well creamed with olive oil and breadcrumbs soaked in water, and sharpened with lemon or tomato juice. It is served cold as a first course with toast. The roe of grey mullet may be used instead of cod's roe.

Tarragon. The true tarragon for culinary use is *Artemisia dracunculus*, a plant with long narrow leaves, soft grey-green in colour; when forced or very young, however, the leaves are bright green. The flavour and scent are aromatic, slightly resembling aniseed. Tarragon is widely used for flavouring chicken dishes, vinegar, and salads.

Tart and **Tartlet.** A case of pastry holding fruit or savoury fillings, without a pastry cover (see PIE and FLAN). Tartlets are individual portions.

Tartar. See CREAM OF TARTAR.

Tartare Sauce. A cold sauce made in the same way as mayonnaise but incorporating hard-boiled egg-yolks. The sauce is finished with chopped herbs, gherkins, and capers. Served with fried fish, croquettes, etc.

Tartaric Acid. An acid found naturally in certain fruits and berries such as pineapple and rowan. Prepared commercially, it may be used in lemon squash made and bottled at home.

Tea. Dried leaves of the tea shrub (*Thea*), originally from China and now extensively grown in India and Ceylon. Tea is divided into two main types, black and green. The principal difference between them lies in the treatment of the leaves. In preparing black tea the leaves are fermented or oxidized before being dried; in green tea they are dried without fermentation. Within these two main types there are many kinds or blends of tea, and all are made by infusion in boiling water. China tea is best drunk without milk in order to get the full flavour, which is more scented than that of Indian tea.

Tea-Cake. A light yeast bread or bun dough baked in rounds. When cooked tea-cakes are split, toasted, and buttered and served hot for tea. The rounds are usually cut into portions, like a cake, rather than served whole.

Teal. A small wild duck in season from 1 September to 28 February. It should be hung from 1 to 3 days. One teal is allowed per person, served roasted with game chips and a green or orange salad.

Tenderize. To make tender. Applied to meat, particularly steaks. These may be beaten in order to break down the fibres or rubbed with a preparation made from papaya or paw-paw juice. If a ragout of beef or mutton is being made, the pieces of meat can be mixed with yoghurt and left for some hours before cooking.

Terrapin. A type of tortoise found in the tidal waters of the eastern seaboard of the United States. The flesh is similar to the turtle's, though the animal is much smaller. Not available in England.

Terrine. An oval ovenproof dish with a lid, averaging 6–8 in. long by 5 in. wide by 4 in. deep. It is intended for *pâtés*, or meats to be cooked with the minimum of moisture. See PÂTÉ and POT-ROASTING. The lid is sealed with luting paste (flour and water) to prevent steam escaping. By extension the word terrine is also used to designate the food itself, e.g. *terrine de foie gras*.

Thermometer. There are four main types of thermometer for use in the kitchen, all cased to suit the purpose for which they are intended:

Bottling Thermometers. For sterilizing bottles of fruit where different degrees are called for, registering up to the boiling point of water (212° F.).

Frying Thermometers. Used to test the temperature of the fat bath, registering to approximately 450–500° F.

Oven Thermometers. Used for roasting and baking, registering up to 450–500° F.; all modern gas and electric cookers have these incorporated.

Sugar Thermometers. For determining the different degrees of sugar-boiling. See SYRUP.

Thickening. See LIAISON.

Thyme. An important culinary herb and one which is included in a *bouquet garni*. Among many varieties the most useful in the kitchen are the common or garden thyme, *Thymus vulgaris*, and the lemon-scented thyme *Thymus citriodorus*; the latter is especially suitable for veal and chicken stuffings.

Timbale. See MOULD.

Tipsy Cake. A firm sponge soaked with white wine and/or sherry decorated with shredded almonds and smothered with whipped cream. Usually garnished with preserved or fresh fruit.

Tisane. Herb tea or infusion of dried or fresh leaves or flowers, e.g. lime, camomile, etc.

Toad-in-the-Hole. Pieces of raw sausage meat put into a batter and baked.

Toast. To toast is to brown under a grill or in front of an open fire. A piece of toast is a slice of bread grilled or toasted on each side and placed in a rack to allow the moisture to escape and so keep the toast crisp. *Melba toast* is a thin slice of bread dried in the oven until golden-brown.

Tomato (*Hycopersicum esculentum*). Sometimes called 'love apple' or *pomme d'amour* in France. The tomato is a native of South America but has long been grown in Europe. In England it is cultivated under glass, though in a good year the fruit will ripen out of doors in a sheltered garden. Tomatoes are widely used in the kitchen both cooked and raw, and through imports are available all the year.

Tongue. Classed as offal. Tongues available are: ox, weighing 3–6 lb. each and usually sold pickled or salted; calf's ¾–1 lb. each; and lamb's, approximately 6 oz. each. The two latter tongues are sold fresh. Pigs' are not as a rule extracted but are sold with the head for brawn-making, etc. See OX TONGUE.

Tournedos. A thick steak cut from the 'eye' of the fillet or undercut of beef. A *filet mignon* is one cut from the tail end of the fillet, and consequently is smaller in size.

Treacle. A syrup produced in sugar-refining. Black treacle (molasses) comes from the coarser sugars, and golden syrup from refined sugars.

Trifle. A traditional English sweet. Trifles may vary a little but the essentials are sponge cake soaked in sherry or white wine, rich custard, fruit or jam, and whipped cream, layered in a glass dish in that order. The cream should be decorated with almonds, glacé cherries, and angelica.

Tripe. The lining or walls of the stomach of a bullock. Tripe is sold ready 'dressed', i.e. cleansed and specially prepared for cooking.

Trotter. The foot of an animal, particularly applied to pig and sheep. Trotters are prepared for stewing or braising, pig's trotters being especially gelatinous.

Trout. See also SALMON-TROUT. A fresh-water fish, commonly found in rivers, lakes, and streams, and varying in weight from 4 oz. to several pounds. The colour of the skin is a silvery brown with speckles, and varies a little depending on the habitat and feeding, as does the colour of the flesh. This is usually white though trout from some lakes are pink-fleshed. The trout sold in shops is a species of rainbow trout bred in specially conditioned tanks. The weight averages from 6 to 10 oz.

Truffle. A tuberous-like fungus which grows underground in woodlands, those from Périgord being especially famous. The black truffle has a rough brown exterior with firm inner black flesh and a strong scent. They are the classic flavouring for, or addition to, *foie gras*. Black truffles reach England in tins and are much in favour as garnish and for adding to entrées. See also DEMI-DEUIL. White truffles with an even stronger scent are found in Piedmont.

Truss. To secure joints, poultry, and game with skewers or string, in order to neaten the appearance of the joint or bird and to facilitate carving. See NEEDLES.

Tunny. A fish of the mackerel family which grows to enormous size. It is caught chiefly in the Mediterranean and off the Atlantic coasts of France. The flesh is white, firm, and meaty, with only a slight flavour of fish. Though fresh tunny is sold widely in many countries it is available only in tins in England.

Turbot. Called the king of flat fish, or the pheasant of the sea. A turbot can weigh 20–30 lb.; the smaller ones, 6–8 lb., are known as chicken turbot. The flesh is white and firm with a delicate flavour; the skin is blackish on one side and creamy white on the other, with a gelatinous texture. Because of the breadth and thickness of the fish it is cut into steaks for selling.

Turkey. Classed as poultry. At one time a native of the Americas but now bred and reared in many countries. In England a Norfolk bred turkey once took pride of place for quality of flavour and size, but nowadays fine turkeys are bred in many parts of the country.

Turmeric. The root of a Singalese plant (*Circuma longa*) which when dried and powdered is used as an ingredient of curry powder. The colour is a bright deep yellow, and the flavour aromatic and slightly bitter.

Turnip. A winter root vegetable which if gathered young is very palatable. The flesh is pure white with a greenish-white exterior and leafy tops. The latter can be served boiled and buttered as a green vegetable in the early winter. Turnips are cooked and served like swedes. Mashed turnips are traditionally the accompaniment to haggis.

Turnover. A PATTY or pie of short-crust or flaky pastry which may hold fruit, or meat, like a CORNISH PASTY. The usual shape is a round of pastry with the filling placed slightly to one side of the centre and the larger piece folded over. The open edges are crimped together before the turnover is baked.

Turtle. A large amphibious animal greatly prized for its flesh, and for its eggs, which are laid on warm sandy shores. The turtle is a native of the South Pacific and Atlantic Oceans and belongs to the same family as the tortoise or TERRAPIN. At one time live turtles were imported into England and kept in tanks, to be slaughtered for City banquets to make the famous turtle soup. This is a clear gelatinous consommé with pieces of the highly esteemed green fat floating in it. Turtle soup is now sold in tins.

V

Vacherin. Large rounds of an almost meringue mixture. When baked they are layered with a *crème Chantilly*. Vacherin can also be rounds of plain meringue layered with cream and fresh fruit.

Vanilla. The dried bean or pod of an orchid, *Vanilla aromatica*. The bean is 4–5 inches in length, and chocolate-brown in colour. When split, it is full of tiny black seeds, which if scraped out are strongly aromatic in flavour and may be added to cream or custard. The bean may be infused in milk, or kept in a jar of caster sugar which may then also be used for flavouring. After infusion the bean may be rinsed and dried and used several times over.

Veal. The meat of a calf. The best veal is that from the Continent, particularly from Holland. Veal calls for special preparation when the animal is slaughtered and Continental butchers do this to perfection. The meat should be a delicate pink with a slight greenish tinge and has little or no fat. The diagram illustrates the different cuts. The offal is also of the first quality; the liver and sweetbreads being generally acknowledged as superior to those of lamb. The kidney also is excellent sautéd.

Vegetable Marrow. See MARROW.

Velouté. Literally 'velvety'. A term applied to a sauce or soup made with the appropriate stock: veal, chicken, or fish. A butter and flour *roux* is made but the flour is allowed to cook to a pale straw colour before the liquid is poured on. After being well boiled the sauce or soup is finished with a liaison of egg-yolks and cream. The stock for a *velouté* must be white, strong (preferably reduced to a jelly), and well flavoured.

Venison. Meat under this heading may be from red deer, roebuck, and fallow deer. The latter is generally park-kept and is considered the best, fattest, and most flavoursome. Venison should be well hung, but, perhaps with the exception of red deer (and this is a personal taste), not in the least high or 'gamey'. Deer are classed as game; the season for buck venison is from the end of June to September, does from September to December. A side of venison is divided into these joints: leg, loin, forequarter consisting of the shoulder and best end of neck. The leg and loin together are the haunch. The other parts, scrag, feet, etc., are not used except for soup. Good venison can be roasted

Veal

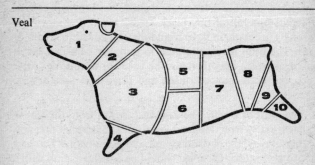

1. Head – *Boiled hot with parsley sauce, cold with vinaigrette.*
2. Scrag end of neck – *Stew.*
3. Shoulder and oyster – *White or brown stew, stuffed, and roast.*
4. Fore knuckle and foot – *Gelatinous stock, jelly.*
5. Best neck – *Chops, grilled or sautéd.*
6. Breast and brisket – *Stews or galantines.*
7. Loin with kidney (best end) – *Roast or as chops.*
8. Loin and chump end – *as 7.*
9. Fillet – *Roast, braised – Escalopes.*
10. Knuckle – *Stews.*

or braised after hanging without further treatment, but can also be marinaded to give flavour and succulence if the joint is inclined to be dry.

Vermicelli. An Italian PASTA, like a very fine spaghetti. Used mostly for garnishes to soups.

Vermouth. A white apéritif made from the skins of the grapes after they have been pressed to extract the juice for wine. Vermouth can be used with advantage in certain dishes, especially with chicken, in place of white wine.

Véronique. Usually denotes a garnish of white grapes. Sole Véronique (poached fillets in a white wine sauce with grapes) is the classic example.

Vesiga. The dried cartilage of the backbone of a sturgeon. It is gelatinous, and after it has been soaked it may be added to the ingredients of a COULIBIACA.

Vichy. The town of Vichy is famous for its medicinal waters, and for the carrots grown in the region.

Vichyssoise. A cream soup of American origin, and made of chicken stock, the white part of leeks, and cream. It is usually served iced.

Victoria Sponge. A cake mixture made with equal quantities of butter, sugar, eggs and flour. A Victoria sponge is used for a jam sandwich, queen cakes, castle puddings, etc.

Vienna Flour. Vienna flour is a fine white flour milled in a special way from Italian wheat. It is used for rolls, pastry, and breads, including Vienna bread which is light and shaped in the form of a long roll or twist.

Vinaigrette. A cold sauce or dressing of oil, vinegar, and seasoning with finely chopped shallots, gherkins, capers, parsley, and vegetables. It is served with salads, vegetables, and some meat and fish, e.g. trout vinaigrette, *tête de veau vinaigrette*, potato vinaigrette.

Vine Leaf. Vine leaves may be stuffed with minced veal or other

181

meat and served with an appropriate sauce; or after cooking they may be put into strong tomato pulp and served as an *hors-d'œuvre*. See DOLMAS.

Vinegar. There are two main types of vinegar: (1) malt, either brown or white and made by the fermentation of malt; (2) vinegar made from red or white wine or from cider. The latter type is considered best for salad dressings and other culinary use, while malt vinegar is used in the manufacture of bottled sauces, pickles, and chutneys. Vinegar can also be made at home by a vinegar 'plant', a fungus-like mass, which is immersed in a large quantity of sweetened water and turns it into a mild vinegar.

Vodka. A Russian 'gin' distilled from grain spirit. Not used in cooking. Traditionally drunk neat with ZAKOUSKA.

Vol-au-Vent. A large case of puff pastry emptied after baking and filled with a fricassée of chicken, mushrooms, or shellfish. See BOUCHÉE.

Wafer. Wafers are very thin biscuits of various kinds, made into various shapes, curled rounds, cornets, etc.

Waffle (French gaufre). Waffles are made from a light batter poured into a specially made iron and cooked over slow heat, first on one side and then on the other. The result is a flat crisp cake with indentations. Waffles are traditionally served with maple syrup.

Walnut. A nut used fairly extensively in the kitchen, chopped or ground in stuffings or cakes, or whole for decoration. The nut is large with a hard slightly rough shell which holds a kernel the two halves of which usually separate when the nut is cracked. Like most nuts the walnut has a smooth outer green case or husk which is removed when the nuts are picked and marketed. Unripe or green walnuts, picked while the kernel and shell are still soft, are pickled first in brine and then in spiced vinegar. Though walnut trees are fairly common in England the nuts that are sold both whole and shelled are imported from France and Spain.

Water Chestnut. Water chestnuts reach England peeled and tinned. They are crisp, and white in colour, the size of a chestnut and with the texture of a Jerusalem artichoke. They are a Chinese vegetable and are much used in Chinese dishes. The flavour is delicate, and the chestnuts need no cooking, only to be thinly sliced or quartered.

Watercress (*Nasturtium officinale*). Largely cultivated in the south of England but rarely in the north (though sometimes found wild). Watercress grows in slow-running, shallow water; and in specially prepared beds when commercially grown. It is in season during the late spring to autumn, up to the end of November if the weather is mild. It is used largely for salads, garnishes, and soups. The flavour is pleasant and slightly peppery. If the cress is good the stalks can be used either chopped or well snipped with scissors to go into a herb stuffing or with the hot milk used for mashing potatoes.

Welsh Rarebit. A form of toasted cheese. Lancashire or Leigh cheese is considered the best for a rarebit, with beer as the liquid. The two are melted together over very gentle heat, then spooned over hot buttered toast and served immediately. It may be passed under a hot grill for a minute or two to brown the top and help liquefy the cheese. The fact of browning, however, turns the dish into toasted cheese rather than Welsh rarebit.

Wensleydale. There are two types of this cheese, one a white cheese which is eaten fresh, the second resembling Stilton, but with green veins rather than blue. Both come from Yorkshire.

Wheat. A cereal grass, *Triticum vulgare*, whose grain is ground into flour or coarser meal and used for making bread, cereals, and pasta products. Wheat is rich in gluten, an albuminous substance essential to the fermentation which produces light bread. See FLOUR and SEMOLINA.

Whelk. A small shellfish. Like cockles whelks are sold ready shelled and cooked on stalls in big cities to attract the passer-by. They are eaten well sprinkled with vinegar.

Whey. The liquid drained from the curd in cheese-making.

Whisky. A spirit distilled from malted barley (Scotch) and other grains such as rye and maize (American whiskies). Whisky has no culinary use, but latterly has been introduced into certain dishes, e.g. hot lobster, in some restaurants.

Whitebait. The fry of herring, sprat, or pilchard caught in the estuaries round the coast of Britain. Whitebait are fried in deep fat until crisp and golden-brown and served with quarters of lemon and brown bread and butter.

White Pudding. This is made and eaten in the same way as BLACK PUDDING, but contains only oatmeal, pork fat, and seasonings.

Whiting. A small round fish of the cod family. The colour is silvery and the flesh white, delicate, and friable. Whiting should be eaten as fresh as possible.

Whortleberry. See BILBERRY.

Widgeon. A wild duck in season from 1 September to 28 February. It is larger than teal but smaller than mallard, and is best served roasted with the same accompaniments as these. See WILD DUCK.

Wiener Schnitzel. Large thin escalopes of veal, coated with egg and crumbs, and fried in butter. Each one is garnished with a fillet of anchovy and a slice of lemon. *Beurre noisette* is poured over them and the dish decorated with chopped hard-boiled egg-white and sieved yolk.

Wild Duck or **Wildfowl.** Under this heading are included such birds as teal, widgeon, and mallard. Unlike most game, wild duck are hung for up to 3 days at most. They are at their best from October to Christmas, though the full season is 1 September to 28 February. Wild duck should be well plucked and dressed, and lightly roasted so that the flesh is a good pink. Some people prefer them very underdone, i.e. SAIGNANT. Accompaniments to wild duck are an orange salad, and a bigarade or piquant sauce. Wild duck also make an excellent SALMIS.

Wine. Though a wine can be produced from most fruits and some root vegetables, that made from the fermented juice of the grape is unquestionably the best. All types of wine are now made in many parts of the world wherever the vine will grow and the sun ripen the grapes, but the wines of Europe are still the most famous. Wine is the best possible accompaniment to good food, and also contributes much in the making of certain dishes, giving subtlety of flavour. See BORDEAUX, BURGUNDY, CHAMPAGNE, CLARET, HOCK, MOSELLE, MADEIRA, MALAGA, MARSALA, PORT, SHERRY.

Wonder. See JERSEY WONDER.

Worcester Sauce. A commercially prepared piquant sauce with a basis of soy and flavoured with spices. Used as an ingredient for devils, etc.

Woodcock. A game bird about the size of a grouse, with a rich, gamey flavour; in season from 1 September to 28 February. Woodcock is a migratory bird and flies in from northern Europe on its way to a warmer climate in October and November. It should be carefully plucked but left undrawn before roasting although if preferred the gizzard and intestine can be removed. The head is also left on, and the beak is used to truss the bird. It is set on a piece of toast to roast so that the juices can be absorbed into it. Allow one woodcock for two people, and serve with the usual accompaniments to game. See SNIPE.

Yam. A large bulbous root with very white flesh and a pinky brown skin. In appearance and flavour it is very similar to a sweet potato. Yams vary in size and colour, but they are cooked in the same way as the ordinary potato. They are grown in the East, in South America, and in the West Indies, and are imported into Europe.

Yeast. Yeast is the earliest form of raising agent or leavening. It is in fact a living plant which needs moist warmth to grow. Once yeast has done its work it is killed by great heat, which is why bread is baked in a hot oven. There are two varieties of yeast: (1) brewer's yeast, i.e. barm; (2) German yeast. Brewer's yeast is rarely seen nowadays; it was liquid and measured by the pint, and could be bought from a brewery. German yeast is drained and pressed barm. The yeast cultivated nowadays is a soft sweet-smelling substance, bought by the ounce from bakers who still bake their own bread, or dried, in packets.

Yoghourt. Milk prepared or soured with a special culture. Though commercially prepared and sold, yoghourt can also be made at home with non-pasteurized milk. The culture or a spoonful of the prepared yoghourt is introduced into milk and kept at blood heat for 24 hours until the milk has set. Yoghourt is used in the kitchen to tenderize meat before cooking, as well as in certain sauces and dressings.

Yorkshire Pudding. A thick batter baked traditionally with roast beef and served before the meat. Nowadays Yorkshire pudding is generally baked separately and cut into pieces for serving with the joint.

Z

Zabaglione. An Italian sweet made with egg-yolks, sugar, and Marsala whipped together. It is served warm in small cups or glasses. See SABAYON.

Zakouska. A Russian *hors-d'œuvre*, which, like the Scandinavian *smörgåsbord*, can be elaborate. Usually accompanied by vodka.

Zest. The outside rind of a citrus fruit which contains the essential oils. The zest should be taken off with a fine grater, or with a lump or two of sugar.

Zucchini. The Italian name of the baby MARROW or COURGETTE. Also called zucchini in U.S.

Zwieback. A German rusk sold in packets. The word signifies twice-baked (from German *zwei*, 'twice'; *backen*, 'bake').

MORE ABOUT PENGUINS

Penguin Book News, which appears every month, contains details of all the new books issued by Penguins as they are published. From time to time it is supplemented by *Penguins in Print*, which is a complete list of all books published by Penguins which are in print. (There are nearly three thousand of these.)

A specimen copy of *Penguin Book News* will be sent to you free on request, and you can become a subscriber for the price of the postage – 3s. for a year's issues (including the complete lists). Just write to Dept EP, Penguin Books Ltd, Harmondsworth, Middlesex, enclosing a cheque or postal order, and your name will be added to the mailing list.

Some other cookery books published by Penguins are described on the following pages.

Note: *Penguin Book News* and *Penguins in Print* are not available in the U.S.A. or Canada

a Penguin Handbook

SUMMER COOKING

Elizabeth David

Summer Cooking contains over a thousand recipes from all over the world – for table, buffet, or picnic. Elizabeth David is well known for the infectious enthusiasm with which she has handled French, Italian, and Mediterranean cookery: she imparts the same quality to this selection of summer dishes that are light (not necessarily cold), easy to prepare, and based on the meat and vegetables in season.

Demonstrating how an unconventional use of herbs can lend interest to the simplest meal, the author describes some forty ways of coping, for example, with the familiar egg, from the Provençal *oeufs pochés* to *Moonshine*, a recipe from the seventeenth century. She is no less resourceful in her chapters on *hors d'œuvre*, summer soups, fish and meat of various kinds, vegetables, sauces, and sweets.

Summer Cooking succeeds in bringing the cool, fresh flavour of garden, fields, and sea into the kitchen and dining-room.

also by Elizabeth David

A BOOK OF MEDITERRANEAN FOOD

FRENCH COUNTRY COOKING

* FRENCH PROVINCIAL COOKING

* ITALIAN FOOD

* NOT FOR SALE IN THE U.S.A.

a Penguin Handbook

PENGUIN CORDON BLEU COOKERY

Rosemary Hume and Muriel Downes

The term 'Cordon Bleu' has come to be accepted as the hall-mark of culinary perfection – the very highest standard of European cooking with a French accent. This Penguin cookery book, prepared by the co-principals of the English Cordon Bleu School, needs little other recommendation.

It is enough to say that it is written for people who like good food, with all that this means. The recipes, for all kinds of dishes are clear and detailed, and the authors continually stress the importance of presentation – of colour, shape and garnish. Equally they give the technical reasons for the methods they suggest, knowing that so much careless cooking is the result of an imperfect understanding.

With this handbook in the kitchen, and herself – at least, in one cunning series of recipes – in the sitting-room, no woman need be frightened of entertaining the most exacting *gourmets*.